FILTHY RICH

FILTHY RICH

HOW TO TURN YOUR NONPROFIT FANTASIES INTO COLD, HARD CASH

BY
DR. RICHARD STECKEL

With Robin Simons,
Peter Lengsfelder,
and Jennifer Lehman

REVISED AND UPDATED

TEN SPEED PRESS
BERKELEY   TORONTO

Ten Speed Press
P.O. Box 7123
Berkeley, California 94707
www.tenspeed.com

Distributed in Australia by Simon & Schuster Australia, in Canada by Ten Speed Press Canada, in New Zealand by Southern Publishers Group, in South Africa by Real Books, in Singapore and Malaysia by Berkeley Books, and in the United Kingdom and Europe by Airlift Book Company.

Book design by Victor Mingovits, NYC
Cover design by Paul Kepple

Lyrics to "My Shoes" © 1986 by Richard Greene, Gunnar Madsen, and Mark Pritchard, Best of Breed Music-ASCAP. Reprinted by permission.

"The Way You Do the Things You Do" by William Robinson & Robert Rogers. © 1964 by Jobete Music Co., Inc. Reprinted with permission.

Library of Congress Cataloging-in-Publication Data

Steckel, Richard.
    Filthy rich : how to turn your nonprofit fantasies into cold, hard cash / by Richard Steckel ; with Robin Simons, Peter Lengsfelder, and Jennifer Lehman.
        p. cm.
    Rev. ed. of: Filthy rich and other nonprofit fantasies. c1989.
    Includes bibliographical references and index.
    ISBN 1-58008-249-1
    1. Nonprofit organizations—Management. 2. Nonprofit organizations—Finance. I. Title.

HD62.6 .S74 2001
658'.048—dc21   00-051146

First printing this edition, 2000
Printed in the United States

1 2 3 4 5 — 04 03 02 01 00

To Shelli, Robin, Will, Traci, Jeff, Jill, Henry,
and the other most precious children on earth:
Taylor, Conor, Aidan, Sutton, and Madeleine.
Leon and Sarah, perpetual teenagers.
Kitty, always there.

to Joan Lengsfelder and Carl Lowenstein,
those eternally youthful spirits.

to Sylvia, Bob, Hallie, and Thurber, forever.

To Zach, whom I will always cherish.

CONTENTS

Picture a Three-Year Courtship
En-Vision the Fantasy
The Enterprise Champion
The Enterprise Team

PART IV—VENTURES: MAKING THE FANTASY REAL

The Current Tax Code
Trade or Business
Business, but Not Taxable
Detours and Shortcuts: Proposed Changes
Relax

    Enterprise Worksheet
    Enterprise Blueprint
    Enterprise Calendar

PREFACE
THE WINDS OF CHANGE ALWAYS SEEM TO BE BLOWING IN THE SAME DIRECTION

New decade, new millennium, same story. The hundreds of thousands of nonprofit organizations that continue to form or continue to serve customers see the same writing on the wall: Be very careful how much you depend on traditional sources of funding. The more you depend on somebody somewhere to give you money, the more vulnerable you will be to the winds of change. Foundation leadership changes, corporate ownership changes, and the cause-du-jour will always change (just five years after the potential devastation of the AIDS epidemic was understood by a majority of Americans, activist and Hollywood icon Elizabeth Taylor bemoaned the apparent reality that the AIDS cause—prevention education, treatment, and the investment in research to find a cure—had become passé).

So, where does that leave you? Are you ready to upset the apple cart in your organization and make enterprise a central feature of your operation? We find that many experienced leaders in the nonprofit sector still don't know how to make earned income ventures and partnerships real in their organizations.

Remember, if this is new to you, you are not alone.

When *Filthy Rich* was first published, the idea of nonprofit organizations earning income through enterprise ventures was a very new idea. Today, thousands of nonprofits sustain their operations with significant contributions from their earned income activities and from profits generated from partnerships with corporations. However, that doesn't mean that this orientation comes naturally to nonprofit managers.

We still, generally speaking, use language that separates the "private," "public," and "third" or nonprofit sectors. Corporations, government entities and nonprofits are defined as different beasts with fundamentally different objectives. That's what we mean when we say that the winds of change still seem to be blowing in the same direction. Every new technology, every new privatization of government initiative, every new joint venture still leaves the nonprofit sector feeling like the poor stepchild of efforts designed for the primary purpose of making money.

So, *Filthy Rich* continues to serve a very important purpose: The leaders of nonprofits all over the world need the tools to know how to make enterprise a vital part of their organizational present and future. Grants, membership programs, donor appeals—these strategies for generating your budgets are all still vulnerable to the game of "who's-popular-now." You need the know-how to take a great money-making concept and make it real.

And, you need the tools to make your idea really appealing. We hope that *Filthy Rich* will give you the confidence as well as the game plan to reap the benefits of becoming a truly enterprising nonprofit.

PART I

NONPROFIT ENTERPRISE: WHO SAYS YOU CAN'T FANTASIZE?

CHAPTER 1
CHANGING THE WAY YOU DO BUSINESS

*The trouble with being poor is that it
takes up all your time.*
—WILLIAM DE KOONING, ARTIST

This book is about changing your nonprofit organization from a poor, grant-dependent, sand-kicked-in-your-face operation into one that is muscular and self-reliant. It is about paying your own way with earned income ventures, and about using those ventures to improve the delivery of your mission.

This book is also about changing the skinny way you think. For too long, nonprofits have been bound by assumptions that limit their effectiveness. No more. A new class of nonprofits has developed, with muscular attitudes and behaviors borrowed from the private sector. The private sector provides some excellent role models—just because they're brawny doesn't mean they're bad guys! So let's throw out your tacit tongue *tssks* right now.

We'll show you how to develop an entrepreneurial nonprofit, one that is goal- and customer-oriented. You will learn how to shape a strong, practical vision. You will see for yourself that your nonprofit can be innovative, risk-taking, and solvent; ventures will earn you predictable and unrestricted operating income. Above all, this book will help you sell your mission—to broader audiences than you've ever dreamed.

LICENSE TO DREAM

Look what other people have dreamed up over the past few years. eBay. Jesse Ventura. Palm Pilots. Britney Spears' belly button! We all got here, to this improbable place of other people's fantasies, through marketing. Still, so many important issues go unresolved while people are out walking their pet Guccis. Nonprofits, especially, seem to be having a hard time being heard.

Why?

Because your fantasy has been weighted down by the seriousness of your mission; your fantasy has taken a bum rap. Some people talk about fantasy as if it were an outdated concept, maybe even a dangerous one, as if it distracts you from reality. Quit daydreaming, they say. Come down to Earth. Get on with business.

In fact, fantasy has lots to do with business—especially yours. Imagining is the business of nonprofits. It is the imagination that sees a more equitable, more productive world. It is the first step toward creating change. How else are we going to feed the hungry? Or cure the sick? Shelter the homeless? Retrain troubled youth? Assist the disabled? Prevent crime? Nonprofits know all about fantasy. That's where their goals begin.

THE END AT THE BEGINNING

Unfortunately, that's also where fantasy ends for most nonprofits: at the beginning. Missions are sparked and sculpted from fantasy, but when it comes to the politics and business of carrying out those missions, nonprofits have traditionally floundered; they can't produce results the way the private sector does; they become traditionalists; they become the invisible sector. Irritating, isn't it?

There are a bunch of transitional assumptions you've been lugging around, assumptions about how nonprofits operate. To show you how universal these assumptions are, we've made a list, and we'll bet you can separate the seven nonprofit grindstones from the others.

ASSUMPTIONS

1. Money will always be a problem.
2. We will always be grant dependent.
3. We will always need some Smokey Robinson and the Miracles.
4. We will always be tied to funders' priorities and schedules.
5. We shouldn't take the pitch on 3 and 0.
6. We can't go back to Constantinople.
7. There will be long lag times between getting a grant and getting the money.
8. Our staff will always be overworked and underpaid.
9. We're dependent on volunteers who aren't always effective.
10. Hawaii is effective.
11. We can't afford to go to Hawaii very often.
12. We can't afford to do projects the way we would like.

Now, let's tally up your score.

If you chose Assumptions #3, 5, 6, 10, and 11, then you've got a distorted sense of grindstones. It's the other assumptions that are limiting your power.

Look at the assumptions again. Highlight them with a yellow marker. You may want to change the world, but assumptions like these—thinking like this—is tying your hands. Thinking like this limits your ability to earn money, to reach new audiences, to adapt to change—to deliver your mission. Believing these assumptions condemns you to live them. It means you'll always be left on the beach or standing in line for the leftovers.

NEW NONPROFIT ASSUMPTIONS

Cheer up. Many nonprofits have learned not to operate under these traditional assumptions. They are becoming productive. In fact, in the last two decades, the Labor Department reports that the nonprofit sector has grown faster than either private business or the government. Enterprising nonprofits have followed their fantasies, and their fantasies have released them from assumptions, have freed them to scout new ways of accomplishing their objectives. You can too. You can decide where you want to go and at what pace.

Take a closer look at your organization and you're likely to find fantasies already floating around, even if you haven't checked them for a while. Don't some of your fantasies look like this?

THE FILTHY RICH FANTASY

- We'll have lots of unrestricted cash.

- The money will be spaced evenly throughout the year.

- We'll use the revenues for projects of our own choosing.

- Revenues will cover our general operating costs.

OTHER NONPROFIT FANTASIES

- We will reach huge audiences with our mission and message.

- We will pay our staff competitive salaries.

- Our staff won't be chronically overworked.

- We will be the best organization in our field.

- We will effect change.

It's time to talk about these fantasies in the light of day, not stash them away as ties to a world that probably was never as good as it is remembered. Realize your fantasies by changing the way you do business, by dropping the onerous nonprofit assumptions and embracing some productive assumptions from the private sector. As Yogi Berra once said, "You can observe a lot by watching."

NEW NONPROFIT ASSUMPTIONS

- **NONPROFITS CAN OPERATE LIKE BUSINESSES.** By adopting for-profit attitudes and behaviors, nonprofits can strengthen the way they operate, the way they serve their customers, the way they meet their goals, and the way they deliver their missions.

- **NONPROFITS CAN HAVE A CLEAR VISION OF THE FUTURE AND A CLEAR PATH FOR GETTING THERE.** By being proactive rather than reactive, nonprofits can anticipate changes in funding and market needs, monitor trends, and plan accordingly.

We're going to assist you in making these new assumptions second nature. In doing so, your nonprofit fantasies will become reality. Your nonprofit can be customer centered, always looking for the next need, with new and better ways to fill that need. Your staff won't have to be underpaid and overworked; by offering incentives and rewards, nonprofits can keep staff motivated and pay salaries commensurate with the private sector. Your audiences are not all poor; by broadening your view of whom you serve, your nonprofit can develop new, paying audiences for its programs. You don't have to wait and compete for funders' handouts. By developing programs that meet businesses' needs you can *earn* money from corporations and put them to work for you. Isn't it about time for that?

Stay loose and read on.

CHAPTER 2
WHY NOW? WHY ME?

The fastest way to succeed is to look as if you're playing by other people's rules, while quietly playing your own.
—MICHAEL KORDA, AUTHOR

Your fantasy is in jeopardy. Never before has the question of your motivation been so relevant. Are you here to effect change or talk about it? For nonprofits serious about their missions, there is precious little time for the gloriously worded mission statements of the 1960s, unless you can back it up with good old-fashioned enterprise. Enterprise must be part of the equation because the only thing that still resembles 1960 is Dick Clark.

NOUVELLE FUNDRAISING

Fundraising was once meat and potatoes for nonprofits. It was never easy scraping together a full plate, but those times seemed halcyon compared with today's nouvelle fare: tiny portions of "greens" served with a sprig of good wishes for better luck elsewhere. The belt tightening of the 1980s followed by privatization of government agencies in the 1990s seasoned an international trend that made it even more difficult to raise money. Yet it's the truly hungry and enterprising nonprofits that make use of these trends. They don't fight them. They relish them.

Here is some food for thought: The following are the forces growling at your stomach that you feel at work....

EIGHT WAYS TO REDUCE A NONPROFIT

GOVERNMENT RETRENCHMENT: With reductions in domestic spending, government continues to cut back on contracts to human service agencies. More than $50 billion over the last two decades, to be exact. Such contracts were the lifeblood of many nonprofits. The decline in government funding forces these agencies to consider cutbacks of their own and to compete with the ever-growing number of nonprofits for private funding sources.

PRIVATIZATION: At the same time that government is stepping out of public service, the private sector is stepping in. Postal service, correctional facilities, health care, elder care, child care, transportation of the elderly and handicapped, Braille translation, and other traditional nonprofit areas are being invaded by private enterprise. As government contracts decline, more agencies are forced to turn to private sources for operating funds.

MERGERS AND ACQUISITIONS: From one week to the next it is difficult to tell which conglomerate owns what start-ups, and which current stock deal will change the economic landscape of your entire community. This kind of business climate often eliminates tens of millions of dollars in grant money. While there is a simultaneous burgeoning of small business, the fledgling companies are not financially stable enough to replace the grant monies lost in the mergers. The result is a slowdown in the growth of the grant pool at exactly the same time that nonprofit demands are increasing. The Fortune 500 may soon be the Fortune 50, and what's more, corporate contributions are flat for the first time in twenty years!

ACCOUNTABILITY: As competition among nonprofits increases, funders are forced to make difficult choices between them. To choose wisely, many funding sources now scrutinize nonprofits more closely. They want to avoid duplication of efforts, so they give money to organizations that have the greatest impact. Unfortunately, giving to the most deserving has frequently meant giving to the most stable. As a result, young and experimental agencies without strong track records are slighted in the grant-making process. To relieve the pressure on their limited funds, some granting agencies have actually begun urging closure of nonprofits with chronic deficits or shaky management. Other grantors lobby for mergers of groups providing similar services. Of course, funders can't force an organization to close, but they can make operation difficult by curtailing the cash.

THE SHIFT TO STRATEGIC PHILANTHROPY: Corporate giving is increasingly becoming a marketing strategy in which companies fund projects that promise the greatest publicity or financial return. Self-interest and *quid pro quo* have become bywords. This makes it harder for nonprofits to raise operating cash and to find support for projects that lack a strong publicity angle.

COMPASSION FATIGUE: Technology makes it possible to view tragedies around the world in real time as events unfold. In fact, each day it gets harder to limit one's exposure to global-scale human suffering, environmental devastation, or cultural depravity. Charities and causes move swiftly into—and out of—the funding limelight. Individuals, as well as governments and foundations, expect simple solutions to complex problems. It's a "flavor-of-the-year" mentality. We gave to that last year, let's try a different one this year—though the problem continues to exist.

COMPETITION OF SORROWS: As competition for funds gets tougher, nonprofits find themselves in a debilitating competition of sorrows. In a world where dollars go to the organization with the worthiest cause, organizations vie to be the most desperate in need, with the saddest story and the desolate eyes on the cover of their fundraising brochure. How many organizations can compete with a children's hospital? It's a competition most nonprofits are bound to lose.

DIGESTING THE HAND THAT FEEDS: As operating costs increase faster than grant dollars, nonprofits are forced to turn to their members and donors for money. The organization adds a midyear fundraising appeal; they increase the price of membership; they up the cost of admission. Sure, the strategy works—for a while. Soon they reach a point of diminishing returns: members and donors grow weary, alienation sets in. The nonprofit loses its most valuable constituents. Clearly, new sources of money need to be found.

These trends compound the existing problems of relying on fundraised dollars: the money is almost always restricted in its use; it is slow in coming with long lag times between applying for a grant, getting approval, and getting the funds; organizations must tie their requests to funders' priorities, often forgoing their real needs and interests; and funding is tied to grantmaking cycles, resulting in uneven, uncontrollable cash flow.

BREAD AND BUTTER BACKERS

To mitigate grant problems, some nonprofits have begun looking to their bread and butter supporters—their constituents. Problem is, many find that cupboard bare, too, because they're looking in the wrong place: the past.

In the past, nonprofit constituents were children of the Great Depression. To them, "Smoke Gets in Your Eyes" was beautiful music and Tyrone Power was the star. To them, money was the valued commodity. They were wooed by the promise of a "bargain" or a "good deal." Nonprofits met this need with memberships, subscriptions, and multiple services at discount prices. They came to depend on those tools as perennial sources of income.

Today's major consumers and nonprofit constituents are careful not to overdo the bread and butter. To them, (cigarette) "Smoke Gets in Your Eyes" is a battle cry and BMW horsepower makes the star. They're baby boomers, and baby boomers are different. With well-paying jobs and double incomes, many of the seventy-six million boomers have considerable disposable income. What they lack is time. Struggling to balance careers, family, and recreation, they value freedom, convenience, and flexibility rather than monetary savings. They will go to the theater for a single performance, but they won't commit to a year's subscription. They will go to a museum when the show is a blockbuster, but they won't buy a membership. Their values and spending patterns are different from past generations. Offers of dollar value that place demands on their time fall on Walkman-muffled ears.

As a result, nonprofits are finding that not only have their traditional sources of grant funding dried up, so have their in-house sources. For the first time we're seeing scores of nonprofits filing for reorganization and protection from creditors under Chapter 11. Some are even filing for bankruptcy.

BEND AN EAR AND OTHER PARTS

The solution is to watch and listen. Then be flexible, use your imagination. Recognize that grant money probably can't be counted on to provide the majority of your support anymore. Creative nonprofits are pliable nonprofits. They are beginning to actively recruit new audiences and acknowledge their audiences' changing needs. That means not only changing what they offer but also the way they offer it.

Several theaters, for instance, are now providing child care with their performance so young parents can bring their children. Many offer dinner/theater packages, so boomers wanting a night on the town can get it conveniently prearranged. Some offer a new subscription model in which patrons advance-purchase a block of tickets—but the nights the tickets are usable are not predetermined. This meets the theaters' need for guaranteed cash and the audiences' need for flexibility.

Recognizing that standard exhibition techniques intimidate many people, museums have begun using more theatrical displays and more live programming. Such strategies help the museums better convey their message to wide audiences.

Recognizing that young parents are vitally interested in their children's education, museums have begun offering more hands-on activities and more children's programs. These additions attract new visitors and build audiences for the future.

Recognizing a Generation Xer's need for an alternative to the bar scene, ballets and orchestras are hosting cash bars before performances. These de facto singles events bring new audiences to the theaters *and* boost concessions revenue.

The key, of course, is not to rely on business as usual. Avoid the head-on disasters that are starving so many nonprofits. Loosen your grip on assumptions and welcome trends as creative advantages. Examine your audiences' needs. Are there matchups that you can offer?

There are salad days on the horizon. The nonprofits above have strengthened both the delivery of their missions and their bottom lines. Their flexible, proactive, market-oriented approach bodes well for their organizations' futures. They have become entrepreneurial nonprofits.

CHAPTER 3
WORDS WILL NEVER HURT ME: CALL IT ENTREPRENEURIAL

When people don't want to come, nothing will stop them.
—SOL HUROK, IMPRESARIO

Who wants to use words like entrepreneurial when there are easier ones to work with? Try responsive. Try customer centered. Try flexible. These are the starting points and should be the core of how most nonprofits think.

You believe your mission must be heard through the roar and clutter of headlines, dot-coms, magazine ads, junk mail, TV commercials, phone call solicitations, billboards, and everything else that bombards us daily. How will you navigate that traffic? How will you get through to people with your message?

Entrepreneurial nonprofits choose the mainstream roads. Traditional nonprofits take the side roads. Who's delivering the message? Let's take a look at two approaches.

MARKET-DRIVEN DRIVERS

Entrepreneurial nonprofits know they must be responsive—and responsible—to their markets. They enjoy serving people. That's where they get their power. They ask their audiences, "What do you want? How are we doing?" If they get off course, they ask their audiences for direction. They are "market driven." They stay flexible, sensing change early, then watching and using it to their advantage.

BUMPER CAR MENTALITY

Traditional nonprofits, on the other hand, are "program driven." They've put their programs in the driver's seat, audiences in the back, and they drive the side roads diligently. Unfortunately, the route doesn't change regardless of who the audience is or where it wants to go. New audiences develop, but steered by their programs, the nonprofits don't see them and can't meet their needs. These nonprofits are captive to the side roads as bumper cars are to an arena.

Traditional nonprofits could "afford" this bumper car mentality because in the oval arena, overhead power was supplied by funders. It didn't matter if the audience tired; invariably there was the grant. Audiences weren't always adequately served, or served efficiently. Nobody seemed to notice.

DRIVING THE DOLLAR

However, funding tightened; now nonprofits need more money at the door. They're faced with fear: Will the dollar drive them? Will it detour their mission? Entrepreneurial nonprofits know that market responsiveness strengthens their purpose; it enables them to serve multiple audiences and serve them better! Their market-driven programs can generate sufficient income to support programs that won't pay for themselves.

Entrepreneurial nonprofits like money rather than fear it. They hire people from the public or private sector who are comfortable with money and who have strong financial skills. "We want people who understand that this organization should be run like a business," says the national vice president of personnel for the American Cancer Society.

Solid financial people know they have to earn their keep. The good ones uphold their concern for quality and service in the face of economic pressure. They turn occasional tensions between program and marketing staffs into productive energy. They use money to enhance the quality and delivery of their programs. They drive the dollar, not the other way around.

VIRGINITY, POLLUTION, AND THE FILTHY RICH

Meanwhile, traditional nonprofits are distrustful of money. Many disagree with the "bottom-line" thinking of the for-profit world. They fear that if concerned with money, they will lose their social goals. They fear money will pollute their mission. They fear they will lose their nonprofit virginity.

Symptomatic of that fear is their avoidance of for-profit terms. The word "profit," for instance, never appears on a nonprofit's budget. Oh no. Instead you see words like "excess over expenses." (Saving money is one area where nothing succeeds like excess.) Local organizations that report to national offices never call themselves "franchises" even though operationally many are. Managers in nonprofits are called "directors" and "assistant directors" rather than "presidents" and "vice presidents."

Even our title, *Filthy Rich,* probably elicits uncomfortable reactions from many traditional nonprofits, as if do-good organizations shouldn't have a lot of cash. Or is it because they think it suggests they've earned the money dishonorably? Lighten up! The useful and honorable in our society deserve rewards, too.

Being afraid of words or money doesn't make sense when you have a difficult mission ahead. You have enough to think about. *If* you become rich, be useful with your riches. Fact is, the filthy part of our fantasy has nothing to do with money. Rather it means getting into the trenches a little, getting a little dirty, maybe even getting a little roughed up because you're willing to take a chance and try new approaches.

Discomfort with money even extends to fundraising where some nonprofits differentiate between "clean" and "dirty" money, refusing to accept money from businesses they don't believe in. Unfortunately, some of the least desirable businesses are the ones that are the most philanthropic. (Imagine the art world without Philip Morris.)

We're certainly not suggesting that you trample your ethical standards in pursuit of money. We *are* suggesting that few financial choices are black and white. As corporations move in and out of industries and countries, it gets harder to remember who's clean and who's not.

Once you believe your mission must be heard through the roar and the clutter, you must be aggressive in pursuit of it. Entrepreneurial nonprofits realize that money is money. It's neither clean nor dirty; it's merely a tool to be used. Entrepreneurial nonprofits control it, not the other way around.

RULE OF THUMB

ENTREPRENEURIAL NONPROFITS LIKE MONEY, RATHER THAN FEAR IT.

RISKY BUSINESS

More than anything, Anita McKeowan wants to be a cop. According to the Orange County Register, she's willing to accept the risks that come with it. Her first probationary year on the force, the Santa Monica (CA) police officer encountered problems in the police academy with a dislocated shoulder and a rattlesnake bite. She also hurt her back and broke her finger while on patrol when she wrestled with a drunk driver who tried to run away.

Six weeks later, McKeowan was stabbed repeatedly in the chest when questioning a man about making too much neighborhood noise. A bulletproof vest saved her life, but her hand was badly cut. A second man put a gun to her head and pulled the trigger, but the weapon only clicked. She was clubbed over the head and sent to the hospital.

When McKeowan returned to work, a drunk driver ran through red flares and smashed into her. After a six-week hiatus and twenty-three days on the job, McKeowan was pulling over a car for a broken taillight when its passenger fired several shots into her patrol car. A wild chase ensued.

In the crash that ended the chase, McKeowan suffered a broken ankle and sternum, a bruised heart, and blurred vision.

"I just hope next year is not like this year," said the determined McKeowan.

If you want to be where the action is, you've got to take risks. Only you can establish the level of the stakes, but one fact is clear:

Entrepreneurial nonprofits are comfortable with risk. In considering a new program or expense, they know that certainty is impossible. After a reasonable amount of research and planning, they trust their intuition and act. This enables them to capitalize on market opportunities. "Whenever you see a successful business," it's been said, "someone once made a courageous decision."

TYRANNY OF CERTAINTY

Traditional nonprofits, on the other hand, tend to fear risk. They want certainty before making big decisions. They have a preoccupation with checking off lists. Since life doesn't provide guarantees, this tyranny of certainty further retards the decision-making process and encourages inaction.

Nonprofits fear risk for two reasons. One is its lack of affordability: They can't afford to lose operating cash by trying new, unguaranteed ventures. Fortunately that's not always necessary. Many entrepreneurial nonprofits have realized that by using the cash of their corporate partners, they need not risk their own. The second reason is a more generalized fear of failure. Trying something new has its dangers, and no one likes to fail. Entrepreneurial nonprofits have realized that failure is just one step in the learning process, one step toward success. They know the only real failure is failure to act at all.

PROFESSIONAL DEVELOPMENT

A manager at IBM was given $10 million to develop a new program. After a year the venture failed. Resolutely, the manager brought his letter of resignation to his boss who replied, "Resign? We won't let you resign. We just spent $10 million educating you!"

STREAMLINED STRATEGIES

Entrepreneurial nonprofits are action-oriented. They know where they are going and are impatient to get there. In order to make quick decisions, they've streamlined their decision-making process so that only people vital to the decision are involved. They are able to compress the lag time between decision and implementation. They've brought together a team of like-minded players who can quickly conceptualize and develop fantasies into practical programs, products, or services. This also allows them to be opportunistic, to watch for and seize the opportunities that appear.

TYRANNY OF DEMOCRACY

Traditional nonprofits, however, tend to be preoccupied with planning. They make decisions slowly, subjecting each decision to endless, and often unnecessary, opinions in a paralyzing tyranny of democracy. Passionate ideas are sucked dry in the process. (See Chapter 33.)

FANTASY VS. *FANTASIA*

Entrepreneurial nonprofits have leaders rather than managers. Leaders have a vision. Through their own passion and optimism, they inspire people to work toward implementing it. Leaders give direction rather than directions. They trust their staff to meet their high expectations, and continually demonstrate that trust. They encourage their staff to make decisions by giving them responsibility and authority to act. They empower their staff by removing obstacles. They manage by asking questions. They listen to the answers.

Leaders see themselves as teachers. They expect their staff to grow, and challenge them to do so. They praise naturally and sincerely, making everyone feel like winners. Leaders are role models for their staff, leading by example. They are not afraid to say: "I don't know," "I need help," or "I was wrong."[1]

Leaders love a challenge—even challenges to themselves. They consider conflict healthy and encourage discussion. But they deal quickly with tensions, not allowing them to fester.

Leaders see both the grand design and the specifics of implementing it. Because they are competitive with themselves, they sometimes set goals that are unrealistic.

Leaders value change rather than fear it, because change encourages creativity and improvement. They have a chameleon-like adaptiveness, meaning they believe the organization would or could change absolutely anything (except for an unwavering set of values).

Leaders have a commitment to value. Value is a result of correctly defining quality—quality products and quality service within the organization to deliver them. Having a commitment to value means that when you recognize you are not delivering full value to your customers, it is time for you to change.

Traditional nonprofits tend to follow a different approach. Just as in Walt Disney's *Fantasia,* wherein Mickey Mouse was the sorcerer's apprentice, staff are often guided by fixed tasks without knowing the eventual goal. Mickey conjured up one of the sorcerer's magic spells and set the brooms to carrying buckets of water from the well into the castle. They kept coming mindlessly with buckets and buckets of water. Mickey almost drowned because of it. Mickey had no vision, and offered none to his staff, so the goal was lost.

> *Nice guys finish last.*
> —LEO "THE LIP" DUROCHER, BASEBALL MANAGER

NO MORE MR. NICE GUY

Entrepreneurial nonprofits expect and demand the best. Being nice isn't good enough. They define themselves as the best in their fields and consistently hire the best staff to help them realize that vision.

Traditional nonprofits, unfortunately, have a second-class mentality. Some say they have an excess number of humility genes. In the name of affordability, they tolerate being less successful than the private sector. They hire cheaper designers for their newsletters, cheaper architects for their buildings, cheaper staff for their programs. The subtle message is that they don't deserve or expect the best, and their staff, public, and funders hear that message loud and clear.

One of the cruelest by-products of this attitude is the willingness to retain under-performing staff. Thinking it's kinder, managers retain people well after it's time for them to leave. The person usually knows what's coming, as does everyone around him. To make them wait and wonder is unfair, irritating, and poisonous to the organization.

The same is true for volunteers. Nonprofits have a tendency to let their goodwill toward volunteers impede the delivery of their missions. They let volunteers slow the organization and lower its standards. Volunteers begin to think that because they're free they can't be fired. A bad volunteer does more harm than good. Don't accept mediocrity, unless you believe you deserve it.

ALTERATIONS WHILE YOU WAIT

Entrepreneurial nonprofits anticipate change. They realize the world is always changing; to meet their goals they must change with it. So they look ahead, they watch for trends, they plan for change, they are prepared. Again, this allows organizations to be opportunistic, to watch for and seize opportunity when it presents itself. Entrepreneurial nonprofits appreciate change because they see it as an opportunity for growth and learning.

Traditional nonprofits tend to fear change. Once they establish their mission, they follow it loyally, without reevaluating it to see if needs have changed. Rather than anticipating change, they wait for it to hit them. Then market changes, funding changes, political changes, catch them unaware. With a thud.

RULE OF THUMB

ENTREPRENEURIAL NONPROFITS ANTICIPATE CHANGE.

SEEING IS BELIEVING

Entrepreneurial nonprofits have a clear vision of the future and of how they will get there. The vision is concrete, quantifiable, and operational; it describes what they'll do and how they'll do it; it defines the style of the organization. The vision is actively communicated, internally and externally. It motivates staff, galvanizes the public, and attracts investors because it paints achievable pictures of success. The vision grows and changes because it is the organization's living definition. It is universally understood, constantly talked about, and frequently challenged.

Traditional nonprofits, on the other hand, have mission statements. These spell out their broadest goals in terms that are unmeasurable and frequently unachievable. ("We strive for an end to discrimination.") Rather than becoming motivated, the staff cowers from the unmanageable task ahead, often unable to take a first step, for the mission statement provides no direction. Nor is the public inspired by such statements: Talk is cheap. As a result, mission statements sit in drawers, unchanged and rarely consulted from year to year. Mission statements are important—but boring. Every organization should have one. But entrepreneurial nonprofits need visions too.

ROAD TO GLORY

All these nontraditional characteristics position nonprofits to take advantage of market opportunities. They enable the enterprising organization to match its skills and expertise with the needs of its audiences; to deliver its programs in ways that are profitable.

These qualities also open a nonprofit to a new, lucrative avenue for reaching people. That avenue is corporations.

You may be used to seeing corporations exclusively as funders, but entrepreneurial nonprofits see and use corporations as something else: as buyers. Corporations can purchase products and services, then distribute them to their own large networks of customers and employees. Suddenly corporations are not just sources of contributions, not even just sources of earned income. They are powerful business partners who, in mutually beneficial ventures, apply their own marketing strength, finances, and savvy to spreading a nonprofit's mission. Remember, entrepreneurial nonprofits

- Like money rather than fear it.

- Are comfortable with risk.

- Have a tolerance for ambiguity.

- Are action oriented.

- Have leaders rather than managers.

- Expect and demand the best.

- Have a sense of competitive advantage.

- Anticipate change.

- Have a clear vision of the future and how they will get there.

CHAPTER 4

USING CORPORATIONS TO ADVANCE YOUR GOALS

PICK-THE-PARTNER GAME

Directions for the game: Match the nonprofit to its venture partner.

NONPROFIT:

1. "UP WITH PEOPLE" TOUR

Performed in thirty-seven cities as a birthday present for company employees and families.

2. NATIONAL TRUST FOR HISTORIC PRESERVATION

Receives licensing fees for duplication of historic wallpaper and fabric patterns found in its classic homes.

3. SHARE OUR STRENGTH

Sponsored a holiday giving program where Internet consumer purchases were linked to donations to the organization. Interest was sparked by users' ability to win two thousand dollars for themselves while generating two thousand dollars for the charity of their choice.

4. NEW YORK METROPOLITAN OPERA

For a fee of $250,000 allowed a new product to be introduced to its upscale audience at an opening night gala.

5. CHILDREN'S TELEVISION WORKSHOP (CTW)

Licensed the *Sesame Street* characters for products that now generate over $30 million annually for CTW.

6. MUSEUM OF MODERN ART (NEW YORK CITY)

Sold the air rights above its building for $17 million.

7. CAPE HATTERAS LIGHTHOUSE

Allowed this partner to use revitalization of the lighthouse in its marketing campaign in exchange for a contribution.

1. Honeywell Corporation
2. F. Schumacher & Co.
3. America Online
4. Chanel Perfumes
5. Bob Solomon/Applause
6. Charles Shaw/Developer
7. American Express Co.

Is it strange to think of corporations as your customers? As buyers of nonprofit products and services? Especially when donation dollars are shrinking? It shouldn't be. Two recent trends in the corporate sector make this seemingly unusual relationship more and more common. Corporate spending is up in the areas of employee relations and marketing.

In both areas, corporations are finding nonprofits profitable beneficiaries of their spending.

EMPLOYEE RELATIONS

Corporations are increasingly sensitive to losses in productivity, especially those caused by employee problems and concerns. Drug and alcohol abuse, child care, care for aging parents, and crime all distract employees from their jobs. To stem these losses, businesses are bringing rehabilitation, counseling, and support services into the work site. This is part of a slowly growing trend to broaden employee benefits, to attract and retain a quality workforce, and to demonstrate corporate concern for its employees beyond the work day. Nonprofits that can creatively offer services to employees can take advantage of this trend.

For example, Eldercare, a nonprofit in Somerville (MA), contracts with corporations to assist employees who have an aging parent at home. Among its services are seminars, telephone counseling, and community resource referrals.

MARKETING

The second area in which nonprofits are partnering with corporations is marketing. Nonprofits, by virtue of their social-serving missions, are endowed by the public with a host of positive attributes. They are seen as unselfish, caring, committed, honest, and a variety of other qualities that vary with the organization's goals. Museums are seen as cultured, high-brow, and distinguished; environmentalists as gutsy and outdoorsy, and as having the courage of their convictions. Additionally, each individual nonprofit has its own list of positive qualities that defines its personality.

Corporations are not so lucky. Their goal is to make money, so they are often seen as self-serving and uncaring—qualities not terribly endearing to customers. Thus, corporations appreciate their associations with nonprofits. In a wide variety of marketing partnerships, corporations in effect "rent" the positive qualities of the nonprofit to improve their image with the buying public. Nonprofits make corporations look good to customers.

In one of the earliest and best examples of cause-related marketing, American Express approached the Statue of Liberty in 1983 with an idea for a donation campaign. The statue just stood there, but her restoration committee responded. During a three-month period, American Express agreed to give one dollar of each purchase made with an American Express card and five dollars from each new card application, to the statue's restoration fund. American Express bargained that by tying their donation to card use, they would make money for the statue and for themselves as well. They were right.

During the three months of the campaign they raised $1.7 million for the statue, and American Express card use rose twenty-eight percent. New card applications rose seventeen percent. The success of the campaign spawned hundreds of similar for-profit/nonprofit partnerships. Corporate marketing departments were realizing the power of association—association with a nonprofit cause. Who would have dreamt? Well, someone did.

In 1998, Starbucks Coffee Company approached Earvin "Magic" Johnson's Johnson Development Corporation with an idea to build their profitability in inner-city stores. Starbucks proposed that they designate local charitable organizations as beneficiaries of profits generated at specific inner-city outlets, with Johnson's company providing assistance in identifying appropriate groups. One Starbucks in Seattle's Rainier Valley donates all profits from the store to a private African American preparatory school. In response to this investment, consumer traffic has increased substantially at this location and an attractive pool of employees has emerged. Starbucks saw a way to build market share among inner-city consumers by associating the company with local nonprofit groups.

All consumer-oriented corporations have the same basic marketing needs.

They need to increase traffic, increase sales, increase profits, project a positive public image, keep their employees happy, and document the effectiveness of their marketing dollars. By strengthening corporations' appeal with consumers, nonprofits help them do each of these things.

HOW NONPROFITS SHINE

NONPROFITS OFFER CORPORATIONS INSTANT CREDIBILITY

Nonprofits are respected as experts in their field. Corporations can tap this expertise by developing joint ventures. When Levi Strauss wanted to promote its line of clothing for preschoolers, who better to work with than Bank Street College of Education, the nation's leader in early childhood education?

In a mutually beneficial joint venture, Levi's paid Bank Street to develop a booklet on hassle-free dressing for preschoolers. Levi's distributes the free booklet at point-of-purchase displays where customers buy toddlers' jeans. Levi's gains credibility and sales. Bank Street gets its educational product paid for at a profit and distributed to a larger audience than it could ever reach on its own.

NONPROFITS HELP CORPORATIONS REACH AUDIENCES THEY MIGHT NEVER REACH ON THEIR OWN

Nonprofits have access to audiences that are closed to for-profit businesses. An appropriate, well-planned joint venture can help companies access those markets.

Public schools are ordinarily closed to corporate advertising. But when a corporation sponsors visits by a Denver Children's Museum traveling exhibit, they are permitted to give a discount coupon to each student.

When B. Dalton Bookseller wanted to promote reading (and therefore book buying), they teamed up with the Public Broadcasting System (PBS) to create a four-year $3 million literacy initiative. Using marketing and community affairs money, B. Dalton funded the PBS series *Reading Rainbow*. They also produced corollary materials for schools and libraries—places that their advertising dollars ordinarily could not reach.

NONPROFITS HELP CORPORATIONS REACH TARGETED AUDIENCES

Frequently corporations want to reach specific audiences—people in a certain income bracket or with particular interests and lifestyles. An association with a nonprofit that serves that audience can help them do that.

When Post introduced its new Natural Raisin Bran cereal, they wanted to attract the attention of people given to a "natural" lifestyle. So they teamed up with the National Park Service. Over a three-month period, they gave the Park Service a percentage of each Natural Raisin Bran sale.

NONPROFITS HELP CORPORATIONS GAIN POSITIVE EXPOSURE IN THE PRESS

Because they are unusual and positive in nature, joint ventures with nonprofits generally attract attention from the media. Corporations, rather than pay for advertising, find their ventures the subjects of feature stories.

When Hallmark Cards sponsored a jigsaw competition at the Dairy Barn, an arts center in Athens, Ohio, the *Today Show* and *Sports Illustrated* covered the contest. Hallmark could not have purchased the positive public exposure with conventional advertising.

ADVANTAGES TO A NONPROFIT ARE MANY

When a nonprofit joint-ventures with a corporation, it suddenly packs the power, reach, and financial clout of that corporation. From that special moment when the nonprofit changes its attitude toward itself and its approach to its goal, new fantasies begin to grow. The fantasies prompt strategies. Within months an enterprising nonprofit can be doing ventures that reach sizeable numbers of people and generate unrestricted income, money that can go toward operating expenses or to cover programs that won't pay for themselves. These are your "riches," controlled by you, not tied to funders' grant cycles or their priorities. The pace is predictable: You decide when and how many ventures you want to do.

Very quickly the nonprofit has three corporate pockets in which to dip. The two new ones, marketing and employee relations, are larger and faster growing than the first. Funding options have increased rather than decreased. The nonprofit is more diversified and less vulnerable financially.

Now, instead of going to corporations for a contribution, hat in hand, nonprofits can come empowered with a business proposition. Building on their own strengths and expertise, entrepreneurial nonprofits can sell a product or service that meets a corporation's need. Unlike fundraising, this is an exchange of equal value, a business deal between partners in which both parties benefit. Not surprisingly, that is the definition of nonprofit enterprise.

PART II

CASE STUDIES

Many nonprofits have begun doing this kind of "venturing" or "marketing." Some are big, multimillion dollar organizations that roll out national programs with major corporations. Others are small organizations with budgets of $50,000 working with a local retailer. Some are doing many projects all at the same time and have started "enterprise divisions" within their organizations. Others are starting with one or two small projects and a long-term strategy. The scale of the projects is unimportant; the principles are the same. They should work for you regardless of the size of your organization, the field you're in, or your location. Here are two examples from very different organizations. What they have in common is enterprise spirit and success.

CHAPTER 5
THE DENVER CHILDREN'S MUSEUM

The staff at the Denver Children's Museum likes to brag that the only worker's compensation claim it ever filed was when the director of public relations wrenched her shoulder during a particularly rowdy game of nerf basketball in the office. Not absolutely true. The museum's driver once hurt his back unloading a traveling exhibit. But that gives you an idea of the playful spirit and character of the children's museum.

If you walk into their landmark bright green building, then trot up to their third floor offices (topped by a purple pyramid familiar to most Denver families), it is easy to be deceived by the chaotic clutter of toys and exhibit pieces, and by the loud banter and laughter. It is easy to think there is not much work going on, and that a host of wealthy benefactors are to thank for this sunny, comfortable space. Not so. The clutter and laughter are actually evidence of the hard work that is ongoing, while the $3.2 million building is a testament to the success of the museum's commitment to nonprofit enterprise.

BACKGROUND

The museum's foray into enterprise began decades ago. After two itinerant "pilot" years, traveling to libraries and community centers, and three years in a dilapidated, ten-thousand-square-foot former dairy, the museum was virtually bankrupt. The three federal grants that made up the opening budget ended and no new money had been raised.

The museum knew the ongoing problems with fundraising: The money was unpredictable, uncontrollable, and slow; the museum had no track record of success with which to impress a foundation; and the competition for grants was fierce. There had to be a better way to fund its operation. The surprise is that they decided to pursue larger, more flexible pools of money in the private sector. To do that the Denver Children's Museum needed to convince businesses to invest in their mission.

They envisioned a museum that was funded by revenues from the sale of products and services to corporations. Those products and services would not only earn money; they would carry the museum's message to a broad audience. Using this approach, they believed that the museum could become self-sufficient and a national force in informal education. That vision became the driving force behind the museum's operations.

The museum knew, however, that if businesses were to purchase its products and services, they would have to get something in return. The museum's products would have to meet business needs. How could a fledgling children's museum meet the needs of both itself and a business? That was the challenge.

VENTURES

LET'S GO TO THE MALL

The museum's first project was a traveling exhibit designed for shopping malls. Common sense told them that malls need to attract shoppers. Phone calls to several local mall managers told them that they spend money to do it. So the idea was hatched for a traveling children's museum exhibit on the arts. The exhibit would be participatory; it would give children a chance to experiment with music, fine art, dance, and drama. Malls could rent the exhibit from Thursday through Sunday, advertise its presence, and attract families. At least, that was what the museum hoped.

They tested the idea on mall managers, and indeed, the managers were interested. Then with potential bookings set, the museum used CETA (federal employment training) money to fund development and fabrication of the exhibit. *Voila*, Sensorium I was born—the Denver Children's Museum's first earned income project!

Over its three-year life, Sensorium made twenty-one visits to shopping malls. Each mall paid $1,500 to host the exhibit for a four-day weekend. The museum netted a total of $25,000.

EXPLORING THE BOOK BIZ

Buoyed by pleasant surprise, new found "riches," and that slightly rowdy spirit we alluded to earlier, the museum took another step: a publication called *Denver City Games*. *City Games* was a book of activities that would encourage families to learn Denver history. Using a $2,300 foundation grant, the museum wrote, designed, and printed the book, then took it to local bookstores. Several bookstores were willing to carry it, in orders of five to seven copies at a time. That was obviously no way to move merchandise. It was slow and labor intensive.

Looking for a better way to sell large numbers of the book, the museum asked itself a question that was to become the bedrock of its enterprise strategy: "Who needs or wants this item?"

Suddenly lights flashed; the answer came from nothing more than an openness to listen to any and all ideas. There it was: Families who were new to Denver were a likely prospect. But how to reach them? Through the realtors who sold them houses. The museum approached the director of marketing at a local real estate company and she bought five thousand copies at a wholesale price. Simple, eh?

The museum had stumbled on a strategic goldmine. In one sale they had sold bulk copies of the book, avoided any risk to themselves, and eliminated the need to spend hours looking for multiple buyers. They had discovered no-risk sales.

High on *City Games'* success, and using the same formula, they produced *A-Maze-ing Denver*, a book of pencil mazes of Denver landmarks that they sold to another real estate firm; *The Frontier Flying Fun Book*, a book on flight that they sold to Frontier Airlines; and *The Babysitter's Guide,* a guidebook on how to be a responsible babysitter that they sold to a bank, a home builder, and a chain of day care centers for use as reenrollment incentive. The museum had discovered the corporate use of premium items—inexpensive giveaways that businesses use to attract customers. Premiums became a staple of the museum enterprise approach.

EXTRA! EXTRA!

Success has its privileges. For some time the museum had wanted to produce a newsletter for its growing family of members. Since it is a children's museum, the idea was to create a paper that would be mailed to the children in each family and contain activities and stories of interest to them. But the idea was stalled because the monthly printing and mailing costs would be too high for the organization's meager budget.

How could the idea of meeting business needs be applied to the newsletter? Easy! Add advertising. But wait a minute, why would businesses want to advertise to the museum's tiny, 500-family membership? Ad rates for that kind of circulation would never support the paper, much less bring a profit back to the museum. Clearly, the circulation had to rise. Easy again with a little brainstorming! Distribute the paper to schools. Give a free copy to every kindergarten through sixth-grade student in the six-county metro area, a circulation of 100,000. Advertisers love those big digits and they pay for them. So *Boing!* was born, the Denver Children's Museum newspaper, the third largest newspaper in the state of Colorado.

Schools liked *Boing!* because for them it was an innovative bimonthly reading supplement that magnetized children on Friday afternoons. Advertisers liked it because for the first time they had access to the parents of schoolchildren. Restaurants, toy stores, and other businesses that catered to families now had high visibility in their primary market. The advertisers put games, contests, and discount coupons in their ads to measure response. They received favorable results. For the museum, *Boing!* was both a "mission" and a marketing vehicle; it brought the museum's creative approach to education into thousands of homes that had never before heard of the Denver Children's Museum.

The staff of the paper was one full-time editor. She wrote most of the stories, recruited staff members to write others, and used the museum's full-time artist for design, illustration, and desktop publishing. Every other month they turned out an eight-page, tabloid-size paper that cost $6,000 to produce. Ad revenues per issue were $9,000, generating a bimonthly profit of $3,000.

MORE THROTTLE

With the *Boing!* editor on staff full-time, the museum became more sophisticated in its development and sale of publications. It developed an efficient system for producing profitable publications in which each book was sold twice. The first sale covered the writing, design, and desktop publishing of the book. The second paid for its printing and distribution. The second sale was always to one or more corporations that used the publication as a premium item.

While the books were designed to be profitable, they also reflected the museum's commitment to educational quality. Each book was activity based. Each took a difficult subject and made it interesting and relevant to children. Each encouraged parent-child interaction. The books were designed to take the museum's educational message to families who could never visit the center in person.

The publication system involved using the *Boing!* editor as manager, and then contracting with professionals for writing, design, and production. This enabled the museum to do more than one publication at a time, and to use a variety of writers and artists to create books with a variety of looks and copy styles. It meant the museum could hire the top writers and artists in Denver because they were hired short-term, and their fees were written into the project budgets. The result was a series of exemplary publications that generated a high-quality image for the museum and its corporate partners.

PET PROJECTS

The first publication to use the double-sale system was *Kids and Pets,* an activity book about caring for animals. The museum was approached by the American Humane Association, which was looking for a way to get its message into schools. Seeing the success of *Boing!* they felt the museum could help. With $13,000 from the Humane Association, the museum developed *Kids and Pets.* The money covered writing, design, illustration, production, museum overhead (rent, phone, utilities, photocopying, insurance, and a percentage of the editor's time, all costed out to the project), and a profit. What remained was to find a corporate partner to print the book and distribute it.

The standard, simple question had to be answered: What business would want a booklet on pet care? Pet food companies, pet stores, and/or manufacturers of pet products. With the book's mock-up in hand, the museum approached several of each. After numerous phone calls and one false lead, they found a buyer: StarKist/9 Lives, pet food manufacturer. StarKist paid the museum $1.25 per copy for 62,000 copies of *Kids and Pets.* They gave twelve thousand to veterinarians, and used the remaining five thousand as a premium, printing a coupon for it on their bags of cat food. Of the $1.25 per copy, 85 cents covered the cost of printing the book; the remainder was profit for the museum.

The museum next produced *Small Change,* a book on money and the economy. *Small Change* was produced for Citicorp, which wanted a premium item to use in its Person-to-Person Financial Network. Citicorp paid the museum a fee to develop and produce the book. They bought 60,000 copies in advance to use in attracting families to their centers. When a Citicorp banker took the book into his son's fifth-grade class, the teacher's rave review sparked a second use. Citicorp purchased 250,000 additional copies to give to upper elementary classrooms in communities where it was building business. By reaching students they were reaching parents, Citicorp's target market.

Numerous publications followed. *Seldom Was Heard,* a look at the real history of the American West, was sold first to an insurance company, which paid for writing, design, and desktop publishing. The company gave copies to a local school district. Additional copies were bought by a local bank whose logo and advertising theme was "the pioneer spirit," and a local department store used it as a back-to-school giveaway. The bank also gave copies to the local historic preservation organization, which used the book as a membership incentive.

Your Children, Our Children, booklets on problems facing America's children, was produced to accompany a PBS television series. Dayton Hudson Corporation contracted with the museum to research and produce the guides, then gave them away to viewers who requested them. *After the Tears,* a book for parents of children with disabilities, was developed with money from the Colorado Department of Education. It was printed and distributed by several corporations as an employee benefit. Later it was sold to a commercial publishing house for national retail sale.

MORE ROADSHOWS

During this same period, the museum began to pursue a second area of earned income, traveling exhibits. Sensorium's success in shopping malls had hinted at the potential of that medium. Now the museum wanted to test it further. The museum bet that given the number of daily field trips to the museum, schools just might be interested in an exhibit that could come to them.

Museum directors tested the idea on school principals at their monthly meeting in a nearby district. There, the museum directors described the exhibit they had in mind: "Colors To Go" would enable children in grades K–6 to experiment with basic principles of color mixing. It would accommodate one class at a time; it would fit in an empty classroom or on an auditorium stage; it would be set up and staffed by museum personnel. Would the principals be interested in renting such an exhibit? If so, how long would they want it? How much would they pay? Much to the museum's surprise, every principal asked to rent it! The principals also offered suggestions on how to make it best meet their needs. Elated, the museum directors took a bold step. They wrote dates on a piece of paper and circulated it around the room. How many principals would sign up for the exhibit now? When the paper returned, they had booked the as-yet-unbuilt exhibit into twenty-three schools.

The next step was to sell it to a corporation that would pay for its development and fabrication. With such strong interest from schools, the museum approached Chevron Corporation. Chevron, wanting to build its public image, agreed to invest in the exhibit for $2,000. That tiny budget and museum ingenuity created Colors To Go, the Denver Children's Museum's first school-oriented traveling exhibit.

When set up, the exhibit filled a twenty by twenty-five-foot space, approximately the size of a school stage or empty classroom. Crated, it fit in the back of the museum's panel truck. It could be set up and taken down in one hour by the museum's driver, and could be used by every class in a school over a two- to three-day period. The museum hired a contract "teacher" to accompany the exhibit on its bookings, paying the person only for hours worked. During its first year of life, Colors To Go visited twenty-seven schools. Each one paid $165 a day. This fee covered the museum's costs in operating and maintaining the exhibit, plus a profit.

After renting Colors To Go, schools clamored for more. Over the next several years, the museum developed a fleet of traveling exhibits on subjects ranging from handicaps to everyday math. Each exhibit accommodated a classroom of children with a variety of participatory activities; each exhibit was accompanied by pre- and post-visit classroom materials, and each earned a profit on its $165/day rental fee. The museum had discovered another winning formula.

As with publications, the formula included using a museum staff person (the director of programs) as project manager, and hiring contract professionals for content expertise, design, and fabrication. This enabled the museum to produce more than one exhibit at a time, and to hire the specific skills it needed at an affordable cost. Concept and execution, likewise, were consistently fresh and diverse thanks to this approach.

As with the publications, the exhibit funding formula included selling the product twice. The initial sale was to a corporation that paid to produce the exhibit. Numerous companies that wanted to reach families paid the museum an average of $18,000 to take their name into schools. That money covered the museum's costs in producing the exhibits, plus a profit. The second "sale" was the rental that covered the exhibit's operating costs, plus a profit.

While designed initially for schools, banks, shopping malls, and family restaurants, other profit centers interested in attracting families rented the exhibits just as often. Even other children's museums became long-term exhibit renters. The museum also rented the exhibits to businesses that would sponsor visits to schools in their neighborhoods. One business might sponsor an exhibit in three or four schools, enabling the museum to make several sales with one phone call.

SPECIAL EVENTS

The museum's third major area of earned income was special events. These were events that created fun educational experiences for families at the same time that they provided targeted marketing opportunities for businesses.

The museum's first special event was the Toy Trade, a pre-Christmas event designed to reinforce to children the importance of sharing with others. The event was held in a hotel ballroom; children brought old toys in good condition. One toy was given to charity, the others were traded for other children's old toys. Families went home with "new" old toys, and several Denver-area charities received a Christmas bounty. The event was based on the museum's formula of "sharing, caring, and greed." Museum staff knew that people like easy opportunities to demonstrate their caring and concern for people in need—as long as they walk away with something for themselves. An event that catered to those feelings was likely to be successful. The Toy Trade was.

A variety of corporations invested in the event. A real estate company, a fast-food chain, a toy store, and a department store each paid the museum $2,300 to participate. For this fee, they became pre-event dropoff points for toys, distribution points for tickets, and were listed as Toy Trade partners in ads and statement stuffers, which they produced. The Toy Trade offered sponsors a way to increase their name visibility and build traffic. The association with a quality event and with a quality institution like the Denver Children's Museum had great appeal to their largest markets. The museum held the Toy Trade three consecutive years, selling it to three partners each year. The event's operating costs were $2,000, producing an annual profit of $4,900. What's more, every event had a media partner, guaranteeing media coverage.

The Toy Trade was retired *before* decline set in. The museum subscribes to the motto "quit on a high," which is good (if not always easy to follow) business sense.

Then they initiated the Parenting Fair. This was a trade show for new and expectant parents. Businesses serving that market bought booth space, demonstration times, and program ads to advertise their products and services. Parents paid four dollars at the door to get in, and spent hours stopping at booths, watching demonstrations, chatting with medical personnel, and learning about parenting options. More sophisticated than the Toy Trade, and considerably larger in scope, the Parenting Fair cost $17,000 to produce. But its income was higher as well. Booths rented for $500, as did seminar and demonstration spaces. Program ads cost $800. "Sponsorship" of the event cost $2,500 and meant a company was included in all Parenting Fair literature and ads. Each year, the fair netted the museum approximately $25,000.

Again, as for traveling exhibits and publications, special events were engineered by one full-time staff person. The museum's director of marketing sold the corporate sponsorships, arranged the event's programs, and hired contract professionals for graphics, construction, audiovisual, and other support services.

RULE OF THUMB

SPECIAL EVENTS ARE REINVENTED OR RETIRED BY THE FOURTH YEAR.

SUCCESSFUL STRATEGIES

Over the years the museum's projects became increasingly sophisticated. Their budgets increased, as did their revenues, and the number of projects surged. The museum was on constant lookout for possible earned income opportunities, for possible matchups between their own educational know-how and a company's marketing needs. How and where did it find them?

It found them by asking itself two questions:

"Who wants what we can do?"
"What do businesses want?"

WHAT WE CAN DO

"What we can do" referred to the museum's wish list: exhibits, events, and publications museum staff felt were important based on their research and knowledge of their audience. The executive director and director of marketing looked for businesses that might want to buy those projects. Simultaneously, they examined the universe of businesses that, because they appealed to families, were potential business partners. They looked at banks, real estate agents, department stores, and restaurants, and asked what could the museum do for them? What kind of educational product or service would meet their needs?

The questions paid off. Five years after the self-sufficiency goal was set, the museum was doing an average of fifteen earned income projects a year. They carried the museum's educational vision across the country as well as across town, and generated approximately ninety-five percent of the museum's income.

PRINCIPLES TO LIVE AND SURVIVE WITH

A set of principles strengthened the financial success of the Denver Children's Museum.

- PRESELLING: The museum never risks its own money in producing a product or event. It presells all projects to corporate partners, and then uses that money to produce the project.

- WHOLESALING: The museum never sells retail to the general public. That way it never wonders how many sales it will make, and never sits on unsold inventory. Instead, it wholesales its products to a corporate partner, which, in turn, distributes them to its customers. The museum makes one bulk sale for which it receives guaranteed cash.

- PRICING: Prices for all museum products and events include three components: the direct cost of producing the project, the indirect (or overhead) costs of producing the project, and a profit. Prices also include intangibles such as perceived sense of fairness, competitiveness with comparable choices available, and mutual satisfaction, sometimes called the greed factor.

- DIVERSIFICATION: The museum believes that income diversification is healthy and that no project should ever provide more than a quarter of the organization's budget. It pursues many projects at one time, scheduled, as much as possible, to provide a steady cash flow throughout the year.

• QUALITY: Quality counts. The museum's corporate partners respect museum staff as experts in family education. That's why they agree to buy museum products. Therefore they are not involved in project development. The museum generally invites partners to look at a book or exhibit during development, but quality control rests strictly with the museum.

THREE MORE SUCCESS FACTORS

Three other factors contribute to the success of the Denver Children's Museum's earned income strategy:

• ALL MUSEUM PRODUCTS AND SERVICES MEET SPECIFIC PARTNER NEEDS. Malls rent traveling exhibits to build traffic. Retail businesses buy museum publications, which they use as premium items to increase sales. Businesses sponsor special events because they strengthen the businesses' public image. Corporations sponsor traveling exhibits in schools and malls because they give them visibility with families. In every case, the association with the museum helps businesses appeal to their target market.

• THE MUSEUM HAS A CLEAR VISION OF ITSELF AS AN ENTREPRENEURIAL ORGANIZATION. This is critical to the development of museum products and services. Since its earliest days, the museum has defined itself as a maverick— young and brash, willing to take risks, willing to make mistakes. Its small, energetic, like-minded staff has a decided bias for action. They have an exuberant, optimistic mind-set—both educationally and financially. They believe learning is everywhere. They believe that what is important is less the subject and more the process by which learning happens. They love the challenge of matching a company's marketing needs with their own educational vision and expertise.

• THE MUSEUM HAS A BROADLY DEFINED MISSION, PURPOSEFULLY. Early on, the museum decided that it was not just about exhibits for children. That is too narrow for an organization that believes learning has as much to do with self-worth as it does with content. In a world of falling test scores and families in crisis, the museum believes that children everywhere need experiences of success. To provide those experiences, they have to reach parents. So the museum takes its mission beyond its building to reach as many families as possible with experiences that promote self-esteem and family interaction.

There is no question that this broad definition helps the museum's marketing efforts. Any business that serves families is a potential partner, and a wide range of products and services are possible. All of them serve the museum's mission to "provide high quality educational products and services for families."

MORAL DILEMMAS

OPPORTUNISM

The Denver Children's Museum's reliance on earned income requires that it be highly opportunistic. This opportunism occasionally prompts accusations: the museum is asked if the "marketing tail" sometimes wags the "educational dog," if it does projects because of their financial gain rather than their educational benefit. Staffers say the museum has never done a project with which it educationally disagrees, or with a partner it feels is inappropriate.

This is not to say that the museum blindly accepts all partners. On the contrary, the programs staff takes seriously its responsibility to challenge any project that it feels is inappropriate. It has done this three times.

The first time concerned an advertiser in *Boing!* Several issues in a row, the back page ad in *Boing!* was purchased by Pepsi. Programs staff protested. They felt soft drinks were not healthy for children, and that it was inappropriate for the museum to promote them.

Marketing staff countered that children see soft drink ads in many places and are fed soft drinks by their parents. The placement of a Pepsi ad in *Boing!* would not prompt children to drink it, any more than eliminating the ad would discourage them from doing so. If programs staff wanted to encourage children to examine the health risks of soft drinks, they could do so more effectively with an article in a future issue. More important, the marketers felt, was that the guaranteed income from the series of ads made publications of future issues possible. The decision was left to the director of marketing and programs, who decided to keep the ads.

The issue raised a serious moral dilemma inherent to nonprofit enterprise. Key to the enterprise system is the relationship between the nonprofit and its corporate partners. Are there potential partners that a nonprofit should avoid? Clearly the answer is yes. Less clear is how to determine which ones. For the museum the answer came by weighing the pros and cons. While Pepsi was deemed okay, other advertisers were later rejected. The museum developed no hard and fast criteria for determining partner suitability, preferring to examine each case individually. "Every organization must find its own bottom line," says the museum's former marketing director. "You have to weigh your image, your constituents, and the goals of the project, and trust your gut about whether a corporation is right for you."

PARTNER INPUT

The second challenge to the museum's educational integrity came when the museum produced *Small Change* for Citicorp. As part of the agreement, Citicorp asked to review the book at various stages of development. The museum agreed. No previous partners had ever asked for changes or input; the review was merely a courtesy. To the staff's surprise, at the first review, Citicorp challenged some of the material. They felt that the museum had not explained banking adequately. Staff countered that the purpose of the book was not to explain banking, but to explain the function of money in a complex system of which banking was just one part.

After several discussions an agreement was reached. The role of banking would be limited to what the staff felt was appropriate, but Citicorp would continue to review the publication for economic accuracy. Unfortunately, every subsequent review prompted similar debates. These slowed the process, the book missed its deadline by several months, and the staff, not surprisingly, grumbled.

Once the book was out, however, and tempers had cooled, the staff willingly admitted that the process had produced a better book. The input of the corporation, while annoying, had in fact, pushed them to find ways to explain economic complexities in children's terms. Left on their own, they would have made the book simpler than it had to be.

This issue raised a different moral dilemma for the museum. This was the first time a partner had demanded input on a project. How far could the museum bend to accommodate its wishes? What they found was that by educating the partner and sticking to their guns, they didn't need to bend at all. They were able to accept suggestions they felt were appropriate, and reject those they disagreed with. The incident reinforced the importance of guarding their educational integrity, at the same time that it taught them valuable skills for working with partners.

STRETCHING THEIR MISSION

The third challenge came when the museum agreed, with some trepidation, to produce an exhibit for the sheep producers association. What educational message could they derive from sheep? They decided to include activities about sheep shearing and the process of turning raw wool into finished fabrics. Families enjoyed the completed exhibit but museum staff felt uncomfortable with it. For the first time they felt they had overstepped the bounds of educational validity. The exhibit wasn't bad, but it was on a subject that didn't merit the time and attention spent. Given the opportunity cost of every project, what other exhibit hadn't they done because of doing this one?

The episode taught them an important lesson. By overstepping the bounds this once, they protected themselves from doing it again. The project made them more careful about which partners to work with, and about trusting their educational intuition as to how far to stretch for a partnership.

The museum minimizes its need to stretch by making its "marketing bottom line" an educational one. Programs department staff are the quality conscience for the institution and projects are not undertaken without their approval. This naturally produces tension between marketing and programs staffs. But the museum finds these tensions healthy because they force constant examination and reevaluation of goals. They promote the ongoing questioning of assumptions, which is a hallmark of museum operations.

LESSONS LEARNED

The museum's earned income strategy has produced numerous benefits in addition to money.

- MARKET ORIENTATION HAS REQUIRED THE MUSEUM TO BE EXTREMELY RESPONSIVE TO ITS CUSTOMERS. It stays in close touch with the changing needs of children, families, and the people who serve them in order to deliver products and services that are on target.

- DIVERSITY AND IMPATIENCE HAVE ACCELERATED STAFF LEARNING. The museum's emphasis on diversity coupled with its staff's impatience has prompted it to do many projects in a short period of time. This has enabled the staff to learn quickly about what works and what doesn't. Each project's experience is quickly incorporated into the next, which accounts in part, for the rapid growth in sophistication of museum projects.

- CORPORATE PARTNERS HAVE HELPED DISSEMINATE THE MUSEUM'S MESSAGE TO A BROADER AUDIENCE THAN IT WOULD EVER HAVE REACHED ON ITS OWN. Broad distribution and the quality required to make it work, enabled the museum to grow in five years from a sleepy exhibit center serving ten thousand people annually to a national organization reaching millions of families.

TRADITIONAL FUNDRAISING

Until recently the Denver Children's Museum had done little traditional fundraising. Foundation grants were used primarily as seed money for earned income products. The museum never did a phone or direct mail campaign. Until the capital campaign for the new building, it didn't even have a development committee on the board. (Even the museum's membership program operated as an earned income venture. The museum packaged memberships as corporate premium items and sold them wholesale to day care chains, toy stores, dentists, professionals, and other businesses that gave them away to families.)

Today, with increased operating costs, new staff, and a thriving Denver economy characterized in part by new philanthropic foundations, the museum has eased its adamant self-sufficiency stance. Fundraising now contributes more than ten percent of its budget. Still, "educational enterprise" is the major thrust of the museum's operations, outlook, and budget. The museum is—if anything—pursuing larger, more ambitious projects. It is undertaking development and design of large-scale projects outside the museum, and using those projects to support museum operations.

NEWEST EXPERIMENTS

POSITIONING A SKI RESORT

In one project, the museum has contracted with Vail Associates to develop a children's center at Vail ski resort. Vail wants to position itself as the ski area for families, and they know the Denver Children's Museum is the perfect partner to help them.

SATELLITE MUSEUMS

The museum has contracted with a local McDonald's franchise to put small-scale children's museums in three McDonald's restaurants. If the centers are successful, the museum will develop a customized catalog of participatory educational exhibits for purchase by McDonald's franchises nationally.

TRICK OR TREAT STREET

In another project, the museum is taking a good idea national. For several years at Halloween, the museum has run Trick or Treat Street, a safe alternative to trick or treating. Corporate sponsors buy storefronts on the fabricated city street and give away educational material and healthy snacks. Thousands of families pay at the door, and between their fees and storefront sponsorships, the museum nets approximately $25,000 each year.

In 1989 Trick or Treat Street went national. For an annual franchise fee, the museum sold the rights to the event to a national fast-food corporation. The corporation arranged with malls and nonprofit organizations in three cities to host the event, and paid the museum's consulting fee to teach the local hosts how to run it. They paid an additional one-time fee for the creation of a Trick or Treat Street guidebook.

That the museum has been able to implement these ventures under new leadership, with new staff and higher operating costs, is testimony to the strength of the enterprise concept. While many factors have changed, the essential ones remain the same. The museum is committed to first-class quality in everything it does. It is action oriented and willing to take risks. It is constantly looking for opportunities to match its educational capabilities with a corporation's needs. The museum subscribes to an entrepreneurial vision in which earned income is a means of delivering its educational mission. Through its attitudes and behaviors, the museum makes that vision real: It lives it.

CHAPTER 6
THE NATIONAL CRIME PREVENTION COUNCIL

At the National Crime Prevention Council (NCPC), enterprise has taken a different route. Rather than pursuing many small projects with a wide variety of corporate partners—as the Denver Children's Museum chose to do—NCPC has developed a small number of partnerships, each of which has produced a large, lucrative, ongoing campaign.

NCPC chooses its partners carefully. It works closely with them to develop both parties' needs. By producing high-quality materials, it has turned each partnership into a long-lasting, mutually beneficial relationship. To NCPC, enterprise is not just a means of generating income. It is a primary means of spreading the crime prevention message.

BACKGROUND

NCPC was formed in 1982 to serve as the focal point of a national crime prevention campaign whose leading symbol was McGruff, the crime dog. The council receives core funding from the U.S. Department of Justice (Office of Justice Programs) and works in partnership with the Advertising Council (the nonprofit arm of the advertising industry) and the National Crime Prevention Coalition (state and national organizations) to develop educational materials, distribute them to millions of Americans, and help America "take a bite out of crime."

VENTURES

In the late 1980s, NCPC realized the power national corporations have for reaching large numbers of people. With local customer bases and national advertising networks in place, businesses were perfectly positioned to help them spread the crime prevention message.

GOING LOCAL NATIONALLY

For their first partnership they approached Southland Corporation, owner of 7-11 stores. Southland was a calculated choice as 7-11 stores are frequently victims of crime, and Southland had already targeted crime as an issue of corporate concern. They had recently implemented an internal crime prevention campaign and had developed ties with local crime prevention agencies and neighborhood groups.

NCPC approached Southland to become their partner in crime prevention by putting McGruff posters and brochures in their stores. Southland agreed. This was a perfect fit with Southland's own marketing and image goals: it positioned them as "a neighborhood store," concerned with the safety of its customers.

Customers responded. In the first two years of the campaign they picked up twenty million McGruff brochures from 7-11's front counters. NCPC and Southland knew they were on to something. NCPC had found a powerful vehicle for spreading its message; Southland had found an effective means of reaching millions of customers with a "we care" message. The two organizations decided to increase the level of partnership.

SAFE AT HOME

NCPC's second corporate partnership was with Texize Division of Dow Chemical Products, manufacturer of household cleaners. Like Southland, Texize was already involved in crime prevention. With products geared to families, they had targeted the area of children's safety and were interested in a national effort to teach parents and children about self-protection.

With this in mind, Texize approached NCPC. The council helped them produce the *Children's Emergency Phone Book,* a booklet on protecting yourself when home alone. Texize offered the booklet free with proof-of-purchase seals. In a companion drive, Texize offered to make a donation to NCPC for every customer coupon redeemed during a specific period. The result: Five hundred thousand *Emergency Phone Books* were distributed. What's more, Texize sold a lot of products and NCPC earned $50,000 from the coupon drive while reaching thousands of families with important information. The two organizations were ready for a second, larger partnership.

SAFE AT SCHOOL

Their second effort was Kidsmart, a multifaceted campaign that used McGruff to carry the safety message to schools. NCPC had developed a McGruff Drug Prevention and Personal Protection curriculum for elementary grades. The curriculum contained a McGruff hand puppet and a set of audiotapes that teach children proper safety behaviors. Through a special deal incentive program, Texize offered to distribute the curricula.

In national media, Texize advertised that for every two hundred cases of Texize products ordered by a store, the company would donate a one-grade McGruff curriculum package to a school of the retailer's choice. For every one thousand cases bought, they would donate a curriculum for the entire school.

Texize also made a shortened version of the curriculum available to parents as a self-liquidating premium. They purchased McGruff hand puppets and audiotapes from NCPC, and advertised them at a cost of $4.99 plus one proof-of-purchase seal from any Texize product. In this way, Texize recouped its cost of purchasing the package from NCPC, and parents got puppet/cassette packages for teaching safety lessons at home. In a simultaneous national consumer coupon drive, Texize also donated twenty cents to NCPC for every coupon redeemed.

The results of the campaign were staggering. NCPC received over $200,000 in donations. Families wanting McGruff curricula at their schools and homes gave Texize its strongest sales quarter ever. At the same time, NCPC reached millions of children and families with a strong crime prevention package.

MORAL DILEMMAS

IMPLIED ENDORSEMENTS

Another NCPC corporate partner is ADT, manufacturer of security systems. The council had targeted rising workplace crime as an important area of attack. They needed a corporation to fund the development of educational materials and help distribute them. ADT, already in the workplace crime prevention business, was a natural choice. So NCPC asked them to fund development and production of a Corporate Action Kit. The kit would contain reproducible materials on protecting children at home alone, on drug and alcohol abuse, on street safety, and on other areas of crime prevention.

ADT agreed and purchased twenty thousand copies of the kit for use as a premium item. ADT distributed the kits through its sales force. This strengthened customer contacts and built company recognition for ADT's local offices. Through the partnership, NCPC reached hundreds of thousands of workers with valuable crime prevention suggestions. They also reached many new corporations, each of whom is a potential partner.

The partnership also raised an important philosophical question for NCPC. McGruff's mandate was to fight crime. If he was to maintain his integrity, as well as his government funding and Ad Council support, he had to steer clear of product endorsement. Could NCPC work with a manufacturer of security systems and avoid implicitly endorsing their products? Furthermore, how closely can NCPC work with any corporation without seeming to endorse it?

The question is an important one that goes right to the heart of the partnership system. It is one the council still discusses, in an ever-vigilant effort to maintain integrity. They feel that their role, and McGruff's, is to talk about crime, not about alarms or other corporate products. As long as they hold to that firm guideline, they can steer clear of implied endorsements. They followed that line in the development of the Corporate Action Kit, wherein security devices are mentioned only once. On a checklist for safeguarding your home is the suggestion that you "consider installing a security device." ADT and NCPC were both happy with the careful wording.

To prevent misuse from occurring in the future, the council established a quality review committee that meets weekly to review all uses of McGruff for accuracy of information and possible implicit endorsements.

The popularity of the McGruff symbol and its potential for misuse have made NCPC realize that they have to be extremely careful in choosing partners. "We realize that partners who gain corporate as well as community benefit are more likely to be long-term allies. The key has always been to choose companies wise enough to balance the two," says Allie Bird, former director of the department of corporate initiatives. "It is essential that they understand our message and that we understand theirs."

Thus, NCPC has learned to scrutinize potential partners carefully. They choose partners already active in public service so the partnership is a natural fit with the company's existing objectives. Both partners talk openly about their goals.

"People are driven by visions of things they want," says Allie. "You have to explore your visions together and find a venture in which they mesh."

STICKING TO PRIORITIES

A second philosophical question arose when the council was approached by MasterCard. Impressed by the quality and breadth of NCPC materials, MasterCard wanted to develop a joint national campaign against credit card fraud. NCPC agreed, and together the organizations produced a package of materials for banks and retail merchants.

The package included a McGruff poster spotlighting five ways to prevent credit card fraud; a statement stuffer on how to protect your cards; and a merchants' brochure and videotape on how to detect and prevent fraud. Master-Card sold the package inexpensively to banks and retail merchants, where it became a hot item.

Impressed with the success of the campaign, MasterCard wanted to do a second partnership. They hoped to extend the fraud campaign with a Spanish-language version of the materials. NCPC was reluctant. While an important issue, credit card fraud was not on their agenda for a major campaign. They were more concerned with rising crime on college campuses.

The two organizations negotiated their divergent needs and reached a compromise. They would do the fraud campaign extension, including a MasterCard sponsorship of McGruff posters for mass transit, which would strengthen NCPC's public identity. Immediately following, MasterCard would underwrite development of materials for the college market.

NCPC had been asked to create a campaign that was not their own priority. They had successfully negotiated a compromise that met both partners' goals, but would they always be able to do that? If not, how far could they deviate from their own goals to develop corporate partnerships? The answer, they decided, is to be very clear about their own priorities, to continually evaluate them, and to choose partners whose marketing goals mesh with their own. At the same time, they have to be flexible. Enterprise is not a game with rigid rules; each partnership has to be individually negotiated. The council trusts its integrity and commitment to its mission. They trust themselves to make the right decision.

SUCCESSFUL STRATEGIES

It's easy to erroneously attribute NCPC's success to their sheer size, national presence, and government and Ad Council support. While those assets help them implement campaigns, they don't help them chart the overall direction that council activities follow. Rather, it is attitudes of key staff that account for NCPC's enterprise success. Primary are their willingness to be flexible and their market orientation. These two qualities have enabled NCPC to see opportunities for partnerships and to grab them.

REEXAMINING THEIR MISSION

From its earliest days, NCPC defined its mission broadly. They believe crime stems from the unraveling of community and the resulting lack of control people feel. Prevention means ending isolation, creating positive role models, and mending broken family and community ties. Defining their mission this broadly has several advantages. It enables NCPC to attack the problem comprehensively, and opens many avenues for programs. Seniors, teenagers, children, crime on college campuses, crime in the workplace, child abuse, drug and alcohol abuse—each becomes a focus for a crime prevention campaign. Each also opens the door for corporate partners. As NCPC addresses the needs of specific markets, they have something to offer corporations that serve those markets.

The list of audiences—and partners—is constantly growing as NCPC researches changing needs. Their attentiveness to the market, their recognition of changing needs, and their eagerness to seek opportunities and act on them have made NCPC extremely effective at meeting its mission *and* generating revenue.

DIVIDING THE WORKLOAD

Remarkably, this range of partnerships has been designed and directed primarily by people in three positions at the organization. The executive director, the director of marketing and special projects, and the director of program development are the primary sales, management, and creative team. This team concept was the brainchild of founding executive director Jack Calhoun and his partners Mac Gray and Allie Bird. Together they and their successors have brought a comprehensive perspective to each venture. As they challenge each other's thinking, ventures are thoroughly analyzed before implementation.

How are three people able to handle these projects in addition to their regular work of running the council? Actual implementation of the campaigns is handled by contract specialists. As at the Denver Children's Museum, the use of paid staff as managers, and contract staff as implementers, greatly increases the resources of the council. It provides a wide variety of skills, spreads management over many projects, and makes possible multiple campaigns that are high quality and affordable. It also enables the council to streamline its operation. The small number of key players, the simpatico nature of their thinking, and their power in making decisions make NCPC fast and efficient. They can act quickly on market opportunities, work on their partner's time schedules, and make rapid midcourse corrections. As Allie Bird says, "There has been an amazing balance of consensus and fast-tracking."

Much of the work is done by NCPC's partners. Once the two organizations have defined the goals and parameters of a campaign, NCPC trusts its partners to develop materials. They guide the process and review all materials before publication. This extends the council's resources, and enables them to take advantage of the professional skills of their partners. NCPC also draws on internal resources. Within the council different departments handle specific areas of crime prevention. Their skills and expertise are "hired" when they apply to a particular project.

The council has systematized enterprise over the years, particularly by creating a separate unit for handling partnerships called the department of corporate initiatives. This reflects the importance of partnerships to NCPC and their dedication of resources to the program. The executive director and marketing director, who are not in the corporate initiatives department, continue to play vital roles in partnership development. As with its work with individual partners, NCPC recognizes the need to be clear, but flexible, in its internal structuring.

THE CORPORATE PARTNERSHIP SYSTEM

Corporate partnership at NCPC continues to grow; its hallmark remains the close affinity between the council and its partners. What makes these partnerships so successful?

Fundamental to the partnership concept is corporate "ownership" of the campaign and its message. NCPC's partners don't just buy a marketing campaign. They buy *into* a crime prevention strategy in America. They adopt the crime prevention issue as part of their corporate identity. They enjoy the feeling that not only are they looking good to customers, they are *doing* good for their country and their communities.

NCPC promotes this ownership in several ways.

- THEY CHOOSE PARTNERS WHO ARE ALREADY INTERESTED IN PUBLIC SERVICE. This way they don't have to convince corporations of the importance of social action. By aligning their programs with a company's existing marketing goals, they integrate "doing good" into "doing good business."

- THEY WORK VERY HARD TO LEARN AND MEET THEIR PARTNER'S NEEDS. As much as possible, NCPC materials and programs help partners build traffic, visibility, and sales, and provide benefits for employees. They also promote good community relations on the national and local levels. While working with the national office of each corporation, they develop variations that can be implemented by local branches.

- **THEY WORK CLOSELY WITH EACH PARTNER TO DEVELOP THE CAMPAIGN.** NCPC knows that people feel strongly about things they've had a hand in creating. At the same time, they need to protect the quality and integrity of the content. That can be a tricky balancing act. "In the beginning," says Allie Bird, "you have to get your mission embedded in your partners' minds. You have to set the parameters of the project—what you will and will not do—and then you have to trust them." This accomplished, campaigns are developed jointly, each partner respecting the other's expertise. Both parties approve final content. NCPC, supremely committed to excellence, zealously guards the integrity of its products.

- **THEY MAKE THE CAMPAIGN AN INTEGRAL PART OF THEIR PARTNER'S BUSINESS.** By involving many facets of their business in the campaign, they give multiple layers of the company a chance to get involved and a chance to benefit. For instance, when Texize promoted McGruff safety curriculums, the promotion involved Texize mass retailers (who sold additional product), and Texize customers (who were given the opportunity to benefit NCPC by redeeming coupons and benefit their schools by buying Texize products).

- **THEY GIVE PARTNERS ROOM FOR CREATIVITY IN THE IMPLEMENTATION OF THE CAMPAIGN ON THE LOCAL LEVEL.** During the Texize campaign, one of Texize's major retailers, Wal-Mart Stores, developed a promotion of its own. Local Wal-Mart stores organized fundraisers to purchase additional safety curricula for their schools. By matching each community's contribution, the Wal-Mart Foundation donated $50,000 toward curriculum purchases.

- **THEY CONSISTENTLY PRODUCE HIGH-QUALITY MATERIALS.** Corporations are impressed by the quality of NCPC's past campaigns, and are rewarded with equally impressive campaigns of their own. NCPC uses the best designers, advertising people, copywriters, video producers, and crime prevention people in the field. They are willing to pay top dollar when necessary because the professional fees are built into their corporate partners' fees. They see themselves as the top dog in the crime prevention field and everything they do reflects that image. Their corporate partners are proud to have that quality and image working for them.

LESSONS LEARNED

DON'T UNDERVALUE YOUR WORTH

The relationship with MasterCard produced another valuable lesson for NCPC. They realized they had been underpricing their partnerships. For as little as $1,000, they had been selling their credibility and expertise to businesses that routinely spent many times that on advertising campaigns that couldn't match a partnership for marketing power. So, the council created the Corporate Partnership Program. Twenty-four corporations signed on as Charter Gold Members. Each has paid NCPC $10,000 for the privilege of working with them to develop a customized campaign that meets both parties' needs.

They also introduced $25,000 partnerships to their old friends at Texize and Southland. The subsequent Texize campaign focused on drug abuse, a high priority for both organizations. It included school kits, computer games, and videos that use McGruff to help kids choose not to take drugs. The $25,000 Southland campaign included a major McGruff presence in 7-11 stores nationwide.

The issue of pricing partnerships fairly is an ongoing one. As with every aspect of nonprofit enterprise, there is no steadfast formula. NCPC continues to experiment with new partnerships and pricing strategies, but they've learned not to undervalue their worth.

HELP YOUR PARTNERS BELIEVE YOUR MESSAGE

Every corporate contact is a chance for NCPC to teach its partners about crime prevention and the NCPC message. Whether discussing a major campaign, approving an ad, or merely having lunch, every conversation is an opportunity to show partners a new angle on the mission. NCPC staff ask their partners a lot of questions. They become familiar with their business. They learn about their personal lives. They look for ways to make crime prevention touch their partners' hearts. The result: emotional investment. NCPC partners come back for more. Many continue crime prevention initiatives on their own. Many bring their business partners into a campaign. This makes for successful ventures and it extends NCPC's resources. As their partners take up the cause, they carry the

NCPC message farther than the council ever could on its own.

Most partnerships don't start at this advanced level. They start with one small venture and grow as partners learn more about each other. NCPC has found that relationships built solely on meeting business needs do not work as well or last as long as those in which both partners believe in the mission. Once that is achieved, the ongoing investment of time pays off repeatedly.

The National Crime Prevention Council has developed its own brand of nonprofit enterprise. Like the organization it serves, it is growing and changing. For council partners, it is a powerful marketing mechanism; for the council, it provides significant revenue and a potent tool for meeting its mission. NCPC partnerships are true win/win situations.

PART III

VISION: CREATING THE FANTASY

CHAPTER 7
KNOWING THE LINGO, KNOWING YOUR VALUE

Like many areas of society, different words and phrases hold different meanings for different people. In this book, we use the words "venture" and "enterprise" more than other lingo frequently associated with this activity in nonprofit organizations. You should know these other terms, hopefully with awareness of how they are often used interchangeably (whether, in theory, they should be or not):

- SOCIAL ENTERPRISE: In its broadest definition, this means any activity that generates profit to be dedicated to a social concern. Tighter definitions address who is being entrepreneurial and why. Social enterprise is not limited to nonprofit managers and their marketing staffs. There are many social purpose businesses run by people who do not live by mission but live to make money...and they also want to make a difference for good in society.

- STRATEGIC ALLIANCE: This is a subset of social enterprise. A strategic alliance is an activity that does not involve your nonprofit coming up with a great idea and then selling it to a corporate partner. Instead, under this concept, a nonprofit lends the value of its brand to a corporation marketing one (or some) of its products. It's mutually beneficial, but the nonprofit takes a more passive role in the marketing activity.

- CAUSE-RELATED MARKETING/PUBLIC PURPOSE MARKETING/SOCIAL MARKETING (TOMORROW, THERE'LL BE EVEN MORE TERMINOLOGY!): CRM, etc., is a subset of strategic alliances. These concepts—and they are frequently used interchangeably—all relate to the idea that you, the nonprofit, or they, the corporate partner, see a way to sell products or services by aligning a for-profit venture with the resources and reputation of a nonprofit organization or cause. When you work together, everybody wins.

- EARNED INCOME: Now there's a phrase you're probably more comfortable with! This relates to the sale of products or services to generate unrestricted funds for the organization.

- SOCIAL PURPOSE BUSINESS: This is an increasingly common design for an organization, based on the idea that a for-profit venture that benefits a nonprofit organization or cause has more flexibility when it is independent of the organization or cause it is working to support. E-Source, the company created by the Rocky Mountain Institute and described on page 176, is a good example.

OK. Now you're hopefully more comfortable with the lingo used by various practitioners of enterprise. But being able to speak the language isn't what attracts corporations to partnership with your organization. It is equally important for you to understand why corporations want to do business with nonprofits. Here are the arguments for both direct and indirect benefits that corporate-based proponents of partnership with nonprofits make to their boards and bosses.

TO BUILD PEOPLE

Direct benefits include building skills in employees, exposing staff to new insights into market needs and opportunities, and helping employees feel connected to their communities. This is particularly important to corporations that struggle to retain good employees.

Indirect benefits of this reasoning include providing access to better educated potential employees, and access to attractive potential employees who value community involvement by their employer. Let's face it; a lot of great people work in the nonprofit sector and their skills are highly valued by many a corporate human resources manager.

TO BUILD BUSINESS

The direct benefits include access to social marketing opportunities and the facilitation of better relationships with suppliers and vendors. Successful corporate leaders are always on the look out for new ideas to make money, and for new ways to keep their manufacturers and retailers happy.

The indirect benefits are access to future new business opportunities, brand differentiation, and the long-term benefits of building healthier economies and communities in which they do business. Think this isn't important? Think again. Building healthier economies leads to healthier profit margins. That is what is proverbially called "the bottom line."

TO BUILD A LICENSE TO OPERATE

The direct benefit of this argument is that partnership with an nonprofit organization is a helpful response to growing expectations that businesses should be socially responsible. Companies cannot avoid this anymore.

Indirect benefits are not really all that indirect: access to attractive stakeholders (including stock owners), access to early warnings of poor perceptions in the community, and progressively stronger positive corporate image and brand positioning. When the brand is viewed favorably, key individuals and groups in a community are more likely to embrace a company that wants to open a new plant, introduce a new product, or repair a damaged reputation.

Here is another way to put it. The reasons that corporations value the opportunity to do business with a market-minded, enterprising organization like yours include

1. To attract, retain, and cultivate stronger customer loyalty
2. To attract and retain good employees
3. To sustain good relationships with communities where they do business
4. To develop a more positive media profile
5. To raise social capital through enhanced reputational assets
6. To improve product launch activities: promotions and launch sales
7. To increase store traffic
8. To more effectively target merchandising
9. To sustain a caring edge: a competitive advantage
10. To build a product brand or the corporate brand

So, as you begin the process of creating your filthy rich fantasy, remember: In the real world, you are an asset. You and your organization are valuable to corporations of all sizes. It helps to know the lingo because they will respect that you've done your homework. However, what they really admire is that you understand where they are coming from and how you can help the corporation achieve its goals as well as your own.

CHAPTER 8
DEVELOPING AN ENTREPRENEURIAL VISION

Show me a man with both feet on the ground and I'll
show you a man who can't put his pants on.
—ARTHUR K. WATSON

Now it's time to roll the dice—to use the theory we gave you in Part I and the case studies we gave you in Part II to form your own enterprising vision. The following exercises are launch pads for meshing enterprise with your organization's goals. As you do them, remember: Enterprise isn't just a means of making money, it's a way of thinking and operating your entire organization.

DO YOU WANT A DATE WITH ENTERPRISE?

If you're courting enterprise, be advised: It's both visible and invisible. It's visible because the ventures you choose are there for all to see, because your partners reflect you, and because your relationship shows on your bottom line. But underlying these outer signs is a holistic vision of what the organization can do and be. Entrepreneurial nonprofits embrace visions in which enterprise is a vital part of achieving their missions. The vision is a living, breathing definition of what the organization does, who it does it for, and how it does it. The vision is cultivated by management, actively shared with staff, board, and public, and is reflected in everything the organization does. For this reason, entrepreneurial nonprofits don't do isolated income ventures. Each venture is part of the vision, one more step in accomplishing the mission.

THE FIRST TEMPTATION OF NONPROFITS

Forget about flirting with enterprise. It's tempting to do a venture or two and say, "If these work, we'll do more." But that's dangerous. The ventures become simply vehicles for making money. You lose the holistic vision in which ventures become vital to meeting your goals.

This all-or-nothing commitment will make some of you anxious, especially in a society where a half hour of concentration is frequently thirty minutes too long, and where everyone wants guarantees though none can ever be practical. But you'll find the long-term benefits of "marriage" outlast the short-term attraction of quickie encounters.

RULE OF THUMB

ENTERPRISE REQUIRES A LONG-TERM
COMMITMENT.

PICTURE A THREE-YEAR COURTSHIP

Your vision is a concrete picture of where you want your organization to be in three years. No more, no less. It is a countdown, a goal you will work toward, broken into achievable pieces. Make it firm, make it measurable. We will show you how in subsequent chapters. Your vision is a series of pictures—both verbal and pictorial—that describe every aspect of your operation. John Sculley, well known for renovating major U.S. corporations like Pepsi and Apple, has said, "The best way to predict the future is to invent it." Forming a vision is your chance to do that.

In the process of developing your vision, you have to dream a bit. Put away the morning memos. Put away every assumption about how your organization operates. You're creating a new organization. For now, anything is possible!

We are not suggesting you create an unachievable vision. Just the opposite! Visions are inspiring because they *are* achievable. Think big, create lofty goals, then break them down into smaller, more manageable steps that you can see yourself accomplishing. Your staff and the public will get excited because they can envision success.

EN-VISION THE FANTASY

Creating a vision is a systematic process. It requires questioning, brainstorming, and gathering information—from inside and outside your organization. You will examine your strengths and expertise. You will study the audiences you serve and the trends that affect them. You will ask, "Who needs or wants what we can do?" and "What can we do for others?"

You will translate this information into a statement and pictures that communicate to your staff, to your public, and to your funders, the direction you are headed in and the dynamism you'll use to get there.

THE ENTERPRISE CHAMPION

To guide this process, you'll need an enterprise champion, someone on staff who understands the concept, believes in enterprise for your organization, and can make it happen. This may be your executive director or CEO, it may be a top manager. Whoever it is must be given the time and responsibility to implement the necessary changes and the power to make them happen.

The enterprise champion must be free to focus on enterprise development. This is serious business, not unusually difficult, but requiring time, commitment, and nurturing. Do not hamper your enterprise champion by expecting shortcuts.

You'll also need an enterprise champion on your board. Once again, it must be someone who understands the concept and believes in it for the organization, someone who can make it happen. Choose someone persuasive who can influence trustees who may be reluctant to try a new direction.

THE ENTERPRISE TEAM

Start the process by creating an enterprise team. This should include two key staff, two key board members (including, of course, your two enterprise champions), and a businessperson who is not a board member. The team will meet several times over the next three or four weeks to do the exercises on the following pages. If possible, hold the meetings away from the office—away from telephones, crises, interruptions. Keep meetings under two hours. That gives you time to warm up, roll, and quit on a high. Beyond that, people's energy starts to decline.

The process should be fun, exciting, energizing, and team building. Share the experience with the rest of the staff. Talk about the process at board meetings. Let the spirit and the laughter of your meetings infuse your new entrepreneurial vision.

CHAPTER 9
ASKING QUESTIONS: A STARTING POINT

As you may know, I have many good friends in the press who, unfortunately, have thus far refused to identify themselves and go public.
—FRANK SINATRA, ON HIS WHITE HOUSE CONNECTION

EXERCISE: AN ORGANIZATIONAL QUESTIONNAIRE

WHY DO IT?

What do people *really* feel about you and your organization? The following questionnaire is designed to elicit information about your organization from a variety of people: insiders who know you well, outsiders who know you through a direct contact, and outsiders who know you solely by reputation.

The questionnaire asks for honest comments on various aspects of the organization. In doing so, it gives people a chance to be creative—to offer their best suggestions for strengthening your operation. It offers them a chance to be critical—to voice the concerns they might not otherwise offer. And it gives them a chance to feel involved—to contribute to your organization.

Their viewpoints should provide concrete suggestions for new programs and directions, as well as insights that you are too close to see. You may not always like what you hear, but if you use the information, any short-term discomfort should be offset by important long-term gain.

WHAT TO DO

Administer the questionnaire to two or three people in *each* of the following categories.

- Staff—key decision makers

- Board Members—those with the greatest influence over the organization

- Boosters—staunch supporters of your organization

- Skeptics—persistent skeptics or opponents of your organization

- Competitors—your organization has them

- Foundations or Corporations—who have given you money

- Foundations or Corporations—who have declined to give you money

- Experts or "Gurus"—in your field

- Recipients—of your services

- Opinion Leaders—progressive members of your community

Bad alibi like dead fish—cannot stand test of time.
—CHARLIE CHAN, MASTER DETECTIVE

Don't prejudice the answers you gather. To get honest answers you will have to ensure confidentiality, so hire someone to ask the questions for you. Pick someone who is a sincere, good listener and who is not connected with your organization. Have him or her conduct the interviews in person whenever possible. Most interviews should take twenty or thirty minutes. Assure each interviewee that completed questionnaires will not be shown to the organization. Instead, have the interviewer present you with the list of questions, each question followed by all the answers given to it. While interviewees' names should be excluded, they should be grouped into two categories: staff and board, and everyone else.

QUESTIONNAIRE

1. What will this organization be like in three to five years?
2. What *should* it be like?
3. What are the organization's top three assets?
4. What are its top three limitations?
5. What three adjectives describe this organization best?
6. Ideally, what should a marketing plan for this organization include?
7. What should it not include?
8. Once a marketing plan is completed, what three factors in the organization will help it get implemented?
9. What three factors will hinder its implementation?
10. What are the "sacred cows" in the organization, the areas no one can touch or change or talk about?

11. What organizations (for-profit and/or nonprofit) do you most admire, and why?
12. What organizations do you least admire, and why?
13. Is there anything you'd like to add?

USING THE INFORMATION

In evaluating the questionnaire, look for consistency in the answers.

- Do insiders and outsiders say the same things? Outsiders may be more accurate since they are not biased by closeness.

- Note the adjectives people use to describe you, your staff, and most of all, your organization. The adjectives will help you define operating goals worth working toward and may suggest new products and services.

- Does your organization have the characteristics of an entrepreneurial nonprofit? Or are there areas you need to work on?

- Is your organization capable of moving quickly on an idea? Once you've developed a marketing plan, will you be able to act on it with speed? Or do you have organizational hurdles you first need to clear?

- Look for potential earned income ventures in the suggestions for an "ideal marketing plan" (Question #6).

- Evaluate your interviewees, using responses to Question #11. What kinds of organizations do they admire? Progressive, entrepreneurial ones whose examples you want to follow? Or organizations following a conventional path? Knowing this can help put their other comments in perspective.

You won't agree with every response, but you should take every one seriously. People's perceptions are real to them, even if you think they're inaccurate. Use the answers to show yourself where your organization needs to change. This gathering of information could be one of the most revealing and valuable exercises you'll do for your organization.

The pure and simple truth is rarely pure and never simple.
—OSCAR WILDE, AUTHOR/PLAYWRIGHT

CHAPTER 10
EVALUATING YOUR STYLE

*I thought Brian was a perfect gentleman, apart from buttering his head
and trying to put it between two slices of bread.*
—TOM PETTY, THE HEARTBREAKER, ASSESSING BRIAN WILSON,
THE BEACH BOY, AT A LOS ANGELES RESTAURANT

EXERCISE: ORGANIZATIONAL STYLE

WHY DO IT?

When you administered the questionnaire in the last chapter, you found a list of adjectives people used to describe your organization. Some were flattering, others may have been a bit messy, or worse. Taken together, the adjectives probably paint a realistic portrait of how your organization operates. Listing them lets you examine the portrait to decide which parts you like and which parts you'd like to change.

In this exercise you'll take the list one step further. You will list adjectives that you want to describe your organization in the future. This second list will give you operating goals to work toward.

WHAT TO DO

1. Call a one-hour meeting of the enterprise team. Using a blackboard or large newsprint pad, make a list of all the adjectives (or phrases) you can think of that describe your organization. Start with the ones from the organizational questionnaire, then add others. Don't forget, accurate adjectives can sting a little too.

2. When you finish the list, think ahead to the future. Suppose you could "fix" the organization in the next three years. What adjectives would describe you then? Make a second list of those.

3. Tell the team the following story. It will help them get started. The Canadian National Institute for the Blind (CNIB) provides support services to the visually impaired and handicap awareness education for

the general public. They made the following two lists to describe their organization.

CURRENT YEAR ADJECTIVES:

respected	sense of humor
cautious	stodgy
underutilized	not well enough known
old-fashioned	approachable
qualified	slow-moving
entrenched	reluctant to change
bureaucratic	

FUTURE FANTASY ADJECTIVES:

dynamic	respected (by clients)
profitable	respected (by general public)
flexible	creative
innovative	experimental
heavily used	loved
efficient	more streamlined
visionary	

Developing the lists helped CNIB in two ways. It forced them to pinpoint operating characteristics of their organization, although they didn't always list what they saw. It made them think about how they want to operate. By listing adjectives for the future, they created operating goals to work toward.

USING THE INFORMATION

The future qualities you have ascribed to your organization will be incorporated into your entrepreneurial vision. Over the next few exercises, the vision will become clearer, as will the path for getting there.

CHAPTER 11
WHAT ARE YOUR ASSETS?

In ancient times, wealth was expressed in many forms. A man might be
judged by his sheep herds, dog packs, or assets.
—LUKE DEEPUR, MIME INTERPRETER

EXERCISE: TANGIBLE AND INTANGIBLE ASSETS

WHY DO IT?

Developing enterprise in your organization means finding profitable ways to sell
your skills and expertise to a variety of audiences. To do that, it helps to break
those resources down into separate components. Individual staff skills, specific
programs, even physical assets such as your building, are all potential earned
income generations.

WHAT TO DO

1. Call a two-hour meeting of the enterprise team.
2. Put six large sheets of newsprint on the walls.
3. Write one of the following headings on each sheet:
   - Organizational Expertise
   - Individual Staff Skills
   - Programs
   - Print and Media Pieces
   - Physical Assets (building, grounds, vehicles, computers, equipment, library, collection, etc.)
   - Other
4. Ask the team to list the organization's tangible and intangible assets in each category. Be as thorough as possible. The more assets on your sheets, the more possibilities you'll have for earned income ventures.
5. Give the team this example to help them get started. The rhumba is an asset to music. No, no! That's the wrong one. Try this one. The Center for Occupational Hazards is a clearinghouse and consulting service on

common workplace hazards. A small organization in rented space, they approached this exercise thinking they had few assets. To their surprise, they made the following lists:

ORGANIZATIONAL EXPERTISE:
• In-depth knowledge of workplace hazards, includinig methods of prevention and treatment, and practical and legal issues

INDIVIDUAL STAFF SKILLS:
• Knowledge of chemistry, labor law, physics, business law, mediation, environmental regulations, politics, and lobbying

PROGRAMS:
• Seminars on workplace safety and workplace regulations
• Consulting services on reducing workplace hazards, on working with labor unions
• Mediation services between management and labor
• Training program for managers

PRINT AND MEDIA PIECES:
• Information and training videotapes on workplace safety
• Booklets on individual hazards and their prevention
• Workbooks on uncovering and eliminating hazards in your business

PHYSICAL ASSETS:
• Office space, 1000 square feet
• Classroom, 700 square feet
• Two computers with database software
• Computerized telephone message machine capable of giving 20 prerecorded three-minute messages

OTHER:
• Reputation for comprehensive, high-quality work, for approaching problems responsively and reasonably, for saving clients headaches and money
• Ability to confer an unofficial, but valuable, "safety seal of approval" to organization
• Access to lawyers, doctors, researchers, politicians

Making the list helped the center recognize marketable assets. Possibilities were:
- renting message space on their phone machine to other organizations
- creating an official safety seal of approval (organizations would pay the center to inspect them in order to earn the seal)
- selling booklets on worksite hazards and prevention to insurance companies to use as premiums for their business customers
- renting their classroom to other organizations needing meeting or classroom space
- selling training seminars on occupational safety to business schools
- selling videotapes and training materials to chambers of commerce and industry trade groups to distribute within their areas

USING THE INFORMATION

Congratulations! Each of the assets you've listed is a potential earned income generator. Keep reading to find out how.

CHAPTER 12
EXAMINING YOUR MARKET AND MARKET TRENDS

If the person is over 40 years old, I tell him he should do something because it is first good for Japan, good for the company, good for his family, and finally good for him. If the person is under 40, I tell him he should do it because first it is good for him, good for his family, good for the company, and finally good for Japan.
—KEN HAYASHIBARA, JAPANESE MANUFACTURER

FADE IN. The room is a third-floor walk-up on New York City's lower West Side. Truck brakes squeal and car horns bellow below. Through thick cigar smoke we see Herbie shifting from one foot to another, like a man waiting for the restroom...

HERBIE: L-look, what about Tidy & Teary, they're a great act. Tidy comes on wrapped in the American flag and Teary throws a bucket of white flowers—

LUPE: The Watergate burglar and the psychedelic guru?

HERBIE: Right! Perfect for our July 4th weekend, so Americana.

LUPE: C'mon now.

[Lupe draws another cloud from her stogie, then releases it in Herbie's direction. She places her left boot on her desk.]

HERBIE: Okay, okay, how about Clarissa the penguin impersonator? Such a sweet person, always a favorite, how can you miss with laughs like that?

LUPE: It's a convention of maitre d's, for chrisakes!

HERBIE: Right, well then, Phillipe, Phillipe the food magician. After he makes his entrance from a bell-shaped chafing dish, he produces then disappears a twenty-gallon tub of potato salad—mayonnaise or German-style, your choice—before...

[Lupe turns away, shaking her head.]

HERBIE: Special deal, single day price for the whole weekend. The man is magnificent with bagel and lox.

[Lupe groans.]

HERBIE: Wa-wait, hold on. The Chiccolini Chimps, now there's a great—

LUPE: Herbie, Herbie. I run a business here. Tell you what, give me Lee Jeffries, the comic. He's funny, he's the best ya got.

HERBIE: I don't handle Lee anymore.

EXERCISE #1: CURRENT MARKETS

WHY DO IT?

You need to know your audience. Traditionally, nonprofits think of their audience as one tidy, homogeneous group. They fail to differentiate subgroups with different needs, interests, skills, income levels, and behaviors. This shortsightedness limits their effectiveness in serving—and attracting—different markets.

A history museum, for example, serves children and adults; history buffs and "lay" people; parents and grandparents; teachers and school administrators; university students and professors; tourists and locals; collectors and appraisers; ethnic groups and people with disabilities...the list goes on and on. The audiences overlap, but each group can be served—and reached—differently.

Segmenting the audiences provides many benefits. It allows an organization to tailor programs to individual groups, enabling them to serve each audience better. It enables them to market more effectively by targeting publicity material to the interests, styles, and emotions of different audiences. It enables them to schedule programs when target audiences can come. Segmenting even provides an opportunity to rethink the fees charged for services.

WHAT TO DO

1. Call a two-hour meeting of the enterprise team.
2. Look at your audiences. Lists all the subgroups you can find.
3. What are those groups' needs and characteristics? How can you serve them differently to serve them better? Ask yourself "what ifs?" What if you changed the times of your programs? What if you changed their locations? What if you offered different programs?
4. Tell the team the following story. It will help them get started. The Canadian National Institute for the Blind (CNIB) had always assumed their clients were low income. So they charged minimal fees for their service, relying heavily on government funding. After segmenting their audiences,

they realized they came from multiple income brackets. In fact, a large percentage were middle and upper-middle class. This realization enabled CNIB to increase their fees for selected services, making some services self-supporting.

RULE OF THUMB

ASK, "WHO *ELSE* NEEDS OR WANTS WHAT WE CAN DO?"

EXERCISE #2: MISSED MARKETS

WHY DO IT?

Nonprofits tend to assume the current audience is the only audience. They fail to ask, "Who *else* needs or wants what we can do?" As a result they miss opportunities to serve and prosper.

Freeze your assumptions about who you serve. You've always served poor people in the inner city? That doesn't mean you should serve *only* poor people in the inner city! There may be other groups who want the same products and services. Maybe they can pay higher prices and subsidize service to your original audience. It pays to look and see.

WHAT TO DO

1. With the enterprise team, study the products and services you currently offer.
2. Ask yourselves, "Who else might need or want what we do?" List as many new audiences as possible.
3. Tell the team the following story. It will help them get started. Swope Parkway Health Center is a walk-in clinic in a low-income neighborhood in Kansas City, Missouri. For years it relied on government funding for support. However, government contracts declined, and as competition from other health providers heated up, Swope found itself needing new sources of income.

As the staff took stock of the variety of services they offered, they realized their modest income neighbors were not alone in needing them. Middle and upper income people also need those services, and in fact, are willing to pay for them.

So Swope opened a satellite mental health center in an office complex. Their strategy was to attract more middle and upper income clients who had private insurance, which pays more for mental health services than the state system.

EXERCISE #3: TRENDS THAT AFFECT YOUR MARKETS

WHY DO IT?

Nonprofits often assume the current audience is the permanent audience. But the world is not stationary. Allegiances change; the fashionable become passé. Technology, scientific discoveries, political movements, weather patterns—all create new groups of people with new needs. The changes may surprise us, but they shouldn't *take us* by surprise. Your current markets' needs will change, but new markets are forming that will need your service.

WHAT TO DO

1. With the enterprise team, look at the changes that will affect your field in years to come. List as many as you can.
2. List the ways each change will affect your organization.
3. List some ways you can take advantage of each change.
4. Tell the team the following story. It will help them get started. The mission of the Vancouver (British Columbia) YWCA is to provide training and support services to women. Their services range from career planning to home economics, from renting inexpensive hotel rooms to running fitness classes. While their charter does not specify a target audience, the majority of their constituents are low income. However, with government contracts and traditional funding shrinking, the YWCA needed broader markets. When they examined trends affecting women, several things stood out.

   - Of all new workers, 60% are women, creating a need for job training and career counseling for women at all socioeconomic levels.
   - By 2031 one-fourth of all Canadians will be over sixty-five. The majority of these will be women, who will need senior support services.

- As baby boomers age, so do their parents. Since most caretakers of elderly parents are women, there is a burgeoning need for support services for caregivers.
- Many baby boomers are choosing to stay home with their babies. These women seek parent education and activities to do with their children.
- The high rate of divorce has created large numbers of working single mothers. These women need child care as well as help creating quality time with their children.

Examining these trends, the YWCA identified five new markets:
- Working women
- Older women
- Women caring for senior parents
- Young mothers at home
- Working mothers

Each of these markets can be served by existing in-house expertise.

Among the new programs the YWCA is considering:
- Parenting classes
- Informational publications
- Informational seminars
- Videotapes

Income generated by some of these programs will support free and low-cost service for the YWCA's traditional audience, women in need.

USING THE INFORMATION

Each group you have listed is a potential new market for your products and services. Keep them in mind as you develop ventures and look for corporate partners.

CHAPTER 13
BRAINSTORMING POSSIBLE VENTURES

A hunch is creativity trying to tell you something.
—FRANK CAPRA, FILM DIRECTOR

EXERCISE: POSSIBLE VENTURES

WHY DO IT?

An earned income venture is a product, a service, or a special event that you create and sell at a profit. Venture ideas come from matching your skills and expertise with market needs, and brainstorming is your chance to get a ton of ideas on the table. Get your most creative, trusted minds together and let them loose for two hours of unrestricted daydreaming.

The process will invigorate you if you don't hold back. Brainstorming is like a mental "walkabout," the rejuvenating treks of Australian Aborigines. As you mentally walkabout, look for importance in everything; nothing is irrelevant; nothing is foolish. As you share each other's ideas, these ideas gain value, they grow, they mature. One seemingly silly idea leads to a "brainstorm." So be prepared to walkabout.

WHAT TO DO

1. Schedule a two-hour meeting, early in the morning (7:30 to 9:30) so people are fresh. Hold the meeting away from the office, away from telephones and interruptions. Tell people they may *not* go to the office first—you want them thinking creatively and long term, not distracted by today's concerns.

2. Invite two key, free-thinking staff people, one key, free-thinking board member, and two or three outsiders whom you value for their creative thinking. (Outsiders are vital because they're not bound by the history of the organization.) Have no more than seven people in all. Give everyone background information on the organization: brochures, the questions and answers you've generated so far, and maybe this book.

3. Designate one person as chief meeting organizer and recorder. Their role is to keep the conversation going, keep it focused, and take copious notes. Your enterprise champion is the ideal person for this job. They must be a good listener because they will be writing more than talking.

4. Start the meeting with rolls and coffee. Give people a few minutes to wake up and warm up, then list your organization's operating adjectives. Make it as long as you can, then look ahead three years. What adjectives should describe you then?

5. That should get you off and running. If the second list is representative of your operating style, what kinds of programs will you offer? What products might you sell? Who will want to buy them? What businesses will want to work with you?

6. Standard brainstorming rules apply: No one can criticize an idea. All ideas are written down. Quantity is as valuable as quality. The point is to get as many ideas as possible on the table. One idea often leads to another.

7. If you get bogged down, ask: "Who needs what we've got to offer?" and "We know who's out there; what can we do for them?" Remember, you've frozen your assumptions about how the organization operates. Right now, anything is possible.

8. The process of brainstorming builds slowly, but by the middle of your session you should be shouting, gesticulating, and interrupting each other as ideas pop into your heads. Quit at two hours on the dot (before the energy starts to lag). Congratulate each other on your ideas. Then have the list typed up. It's the job of the enterprise champion to prioritize the list later. Don't be surprised: You'll have more ideas than you'll be able to use.

USING THE INFORMATION

See Chapter 20.

"Nothing is more dangerous than an idea when it is the only one you have."
—EMILE CHARTIER, PHILOSOPHER

CHAPTER 14
DEFINING YOUR FUTURE

*More and more these days I find myself pondering how to reconcile my
net income with my gross habits.*
—JOHN KIRK NELSON

EXERCISE: FLESH OUT YOUR FANTASY

WHY DO IT?

In "Evaluating Your Style" (Chapter 10) you defined your organization's future
operating style. In "Examining Your Markets and Market Trends" (Chapter 12)
you found new audiences for your programs. "Brainstorming Possible Ventures"
(Chapter 13) gave you a list of projects you might offer. The picture of your new
entrepreneurial organization is taking shape.

Now let's add some weight. There are many other aspects of your organization that you want to control: finances, building, staffing, public image....All
these will influence your ability to deliver your mission in the most effective way.
By defining goals in these areas now, you clarify your vision. You start making
your fantasy real.

The following exercise asks you to describe how your organization will
look and feel to insiders and outsiders, and to overlay that information on the
programs, markets, and operating characteristics you have already defined. It asks
you to create a holistic, concrete vision of your organization three years from now.

Why three years? Three years allows you enough time to engineer significant changes yet it's close enough for everyone to set their sights on. There's an
urgency in three years that will keep your momentum going once you start
moving toward these goals.

WHAT TO DO

1. Hold a two-hour meeting of the enterprise team.
2. Hire an illustrator to attend the meeting. He or she will hear the "raw"
   emotional concepts of your organization and will be able to give shape to

them in simple sketches. These renderings will become important communication tools.

3. Imagine it's four years from now. Look back on year three and answer the questions on the next page.

4. As you answer them, think big! Freeze your assumptions about your organization's limitations; let your excitement and imagination carry your goals farther than they might otherwise go. Don't just say you'll break even; say you'll have money in a cash reserve. Don't just say you'll have more visitors than you have now; say you'll double your attendance. Remember that, unlike the traditional nonprofit, entrepreneurial organizations always push their limits and challenge their own expectations. Think creatively now, or you'll never achieve big goals.

5. At the same time, be realistic; you need a future vision that is grounded in reality. Do this by creating a logical extension of who you are now. Push your limits, but give yourself time. Don't promise too much too soon. Your vision should be achievable in incremental steps. You must see the path to getting there and you must be able to make your constituents and investors see it too. Your constituents will need to believe in your organization if they are to ride through your changes with you. They should be your proudest boosters as you grow. Investors are vital because you need them to launch ventures; you can't do it without them.

6. To paint a picture that is big *and* realistic, answer the following questions in the past tense. Talking about what you have already accomplished will keep you pegged to reality.

7. Make your answers quantifiable. Include measurable proof of your accomplishments. Don't just say you had money in a cash reserve; say how much you had in the reserve. Don't say your staff liked working there; give evidence that was so. Is turnover measurably lower? How much lower? Are salaries measurably higher? How much higher? By quantifying your goals, you can measure your progress toward them.

8. Develop a vision with teeth: bring a new businessperson into the process. Ask someone who isn't a board member, who will bring all his or her business sense to bear on the situation. Tell him or her that their job is to play the role of skeptic, or better yet, the role of potential investor. As you go through the questions, their job is to challenge every answer; to push for

the kind of answers he or she would want if they were considering putting $250,000 into your organization and expected a return. Pick someone caring, but tell them not to be kind. They must be honest, insistent—almost irritating—if they want to help you.

> *Where there is no truth, there is no kindness.*
> —NACHMAN OF BRATSLAV, ARDENT 18TH-CENTURY CABALIST AND ASCETIC

THIRD-YEAR QUESTIONS

Imagine it's four years from now. Look back at year three and answer these questions.

1. You received three fan letters from customers. Where did they go?
2. *Fortune* magazine cited a major accomplishment of yours. What did it say?
3. The mayor of your city cited a major accomplishment. What was it?
4. What did your balance sheet look like?
5. Your calendar was filled with appointments in year three. With whom did you meet?
6. You added five new board members. Who were they?
7. Describe your physical space.
8. One CEO of a major corporation turns to another and says, "Imagine that! That organization actually _____!" What did he or she say?
9. A major foundation head gives a speech that begins, "I didn't think this was possible, but *(your organization)* actually did _____." What achievement is he or she extolling?
10. What were your major activities of the year?
11. Who were the customers for each activity, and how many were there? What did you charge them?
12. Draw your staff organization chart.
13. At your year-end profit-sharing party, the staff gave testimonials to what they like about the organization. What did they say?

USING THE INFORMATION

By answering these questions, you've put a lot of flesh on the fantasy of your new entrepreneurial organization; you've made it less a fantasy and more a realizable vision.

CHAPTER 15
THE PROMISE ONLY YOU CAN MAKE

*In 1985 a Rochester (NY) supermarket chain advertised for
"part-time career associate scanning professionals." In other words,
they were hiring checkout clerks.*

EXERCISE: LIST OF ONLYS

WHY DO IT?

Your vision is not only a picture of the things you'll do in the future. It's a positioning statement. It's a definition of the things you do better than anyone else. In your crowded field of endeavor, it's the reason people come to you.

We live in an age of specialization. Doctors are no longer general practitioners; they are internists, cardiologists, or other specialists. Sneakers are no longer all-purpose sports shoes; they are running shoes, tennis shoes, basketball shoes, aerobics shoes, each specialized to the demands of an individual sport.

Even department stores, which once dominated merchandising with their offers of something for everyone, are now carved into specialty stores within stores. How else to compete with the plethora of specialty boutiques that offer just one kind of merchandise but in every conceivable shape, color, and size? It's no longer credible to offer something for everyone. Consumers demand the depth, quality, and quantity that specialization brings.

To succeed, that specialization must be promoted. It must become inherent to the image of the product or business; it must become the reason consumers want to use it. Successful businesses are good at this.

As an example, Scandinavian Airline Systems (SAS) could have marketed itself as "the best airline in Europe." But that would have been a grandiose, unbelievable claim. Instead, it decided to be "the best airline for frequent business travelers in Europe." SAS picked a targeted audience with definable needs, changed its way of doing business to meet those needs, and then marketed its ability to those people.

A less substantive approach might be Proctor and Gamble's. They could have marketed Wisk as "the best all-purpose laundry detergent." But that claim is so broad it becomes bland and unbelievable. Instead, they sell its ability to eliminate "ring around the collar." By targeting a specific, recognizable need, they create credibility and desire for their product. Soiled collars remain and Wisk sells.

The same opportunities are available to nonprofits. Specialization sells. Quality specialization endures. To attract customers, you need to do one or two things and do them well. Whatever your field, you need to single yourself out from your competition by being the best in your area of specialty.

WHAT TO DO

1. Hold a two-hour meeting of the enterprise team.
2. Make sure your professional skeptic is there.
3. Define your area of specialty, the one or two areas in which you will set the standard for your field. Ask yourselves:
   - What do you do that no one else does?
   - What do you do better than anyone else?
   - Why will people come to you instead of to your competition?
   - What is the promise only you can make?
4. Tell the team the following story. It will help them get started. Swope Parkway Health Center, the Kansas City comprehensive health clinic in the low-income neighborhood, had failing attendance rates and a reputation for low staff morale and long waiting times. As part of an overall plan to strengthen the organization, they decided not to be all things to all people, but to serve their immediate neighborhood very well. They initiated a publicly advertised policy of "Dignity Care" in which they offer the kinds of service people expect from expensive private hospitals: guaranteed minimum waiting times, valet service, and roses for all new mothers. Behind the new policy is Swope's positioning statement: They now define themselves as "the best health clinic for modest-income people."

USING THE INFORMATION

You will use this information to shape the slogan and visuals that will describe your organization to the public.

CHAPTER 16
COMMUNICATING THE VISION

EXERCISE: CREATE A SLOGAN AND VISUALS

WHY DO IT?

You've developed a vision of who you are, what you do, whom you do it for, and why you're the best in your field. Now you need to communicate that vision. You need to tell partners who will invest in your ventures, audiences who will use your products and services, constituents who need to understand how and why you are changing, and staff and board members who need to be educated about the organization's goals and directions. You need strong, clear sales tools that will keep your purpose visible even when you can't be there in person.

WHAT TO DO

1. Start by writing statements you think reflect your vision. Write them several ways until you come up with one that says it all. (Remember, this isn't a mission statement. Mission statements are like personnel policies, important, but boring. They help the staff but don't inspire the public. You want a statement that tells your public you've got what they want.)

2. When you get a statement you like, take it to a professional copywriter. Explain your vision, your audiences, and what you need the statement to achieve. Ask him or her to put some "sizzle" in your slogan. Take time to look at various copywriters' portfolios to substantiate each person's experience and talent, and do not underestimate the value of professionals who have spent years honing their craft.

3. If you have not already done so (Chapter 14), hire an illustrator to translate your verbal pictures into drawings. Choose your illustrator with the same care that you did your writer. You've been "painting" your vision all along. Now it's time to put it on paper so other people can see it too.

4. Pick up to five venture ideas that typify the "new you" and explain them to the illustrator. Ask him or her to draw the activities in use.

    If, for example, you'll be producing educational books for families, have him draw families enjoying the books together. Make sure the titles, subjects, and your organization's name are quickly visible.

If you'll be developing exhibits for shopping malls, show people using an exhibit in a mall. Always make sure your name and the subject are visible. It doesn't matter if you don't know the exhibit's content yet. You know enough about your field and the exhibit's goals to make an educated guess. The drawings can be simple black-and-white renderings. They don't need to be fancy. They do need to be legible and professional.

5. Before you release the artist and copywriter, test your slogan and pictures on three potential users of your products and services. Ask each one:
   - Would you use us?
   - How much would you pay?
   - How will you be different afterward?

   Test the pictures and slogan on potential investors and colleagues, too. If you don't get the desired responses, change them until you do.

USING THE INFORMATION

THE SLOGAN

Adopt the slogan as a tag line to your name. Put it on your stationery and business cards. Add it to your logo. It should tell the public in one crisp sentence what you are about, so use it to promote your mission and message wherever people see your name.

THE VISUALS

Include them in funding proposals to teach corporations and foundations about your organization. Include them in your newsletter to tell members where you are going. Use them in promotional materials that describe your goals. Include them in press packets. Use them to recruit board members. Blow them up to sixteen by twenty inches, mount them on foamcore, and use them in-house to show to staff, board, and visitors.

Together, your slogan and pictures will be your principal sales tool for communicating your vision to the public and investors. Boldly and quickly they should say: This is who we are. We're focused in our vision. We're entrepreneurial in our outlook. We're not like any other nonprofit you know.

FROM STATEMENTS TO SLOGANS

ORGANIZATION: Institute for Nonprofit Organization Management, a nonprofit management consulting firm

THEIR VISION STATEMENT: We are the national resource for informed nonprofit decision-makers who are striving for organizational effectiveness.

THEIR FINAL SLOGAN: We specialize in nonprofit turnarounds.

ORGANIZATION: AddVenture Network, a nonprofit marketing consulting firm

THEIR VISION STATEMENT: We develop marketing strategies, products, and services that diversify nonprofits' income.

THEIR FINAL SLOGAN: We change the way nonprofits do business.

ORGANIZATION: Swim B.C., a recreational and competitive swim center

THEIR VISION STATEMENT: To generate revenue and resources to support the goals and objectives of selected sport and recreation agencies through worldwide leadership in the development of aquatic products, services, and education.

THEIR FINAL SLOGAN: We are your competitive edge.

CHAPTER 17
UPDATING YOUR FANTASY

Mussolini had a clear, inflexible vision of himself that not even Heaven could alter. On arriving there, he found only one mirror that everyone had to share. The waiting line was endless. Undaunted, Mussolini strode to the front and pushed aside Napoleon who was buttoning his tunic.

"I am the Duce," intoned Mussolini.

"I am Caesar," called a voice from behind. "Yet I have the patience to wait."

"Not I!" said Mussolini.

Those in line began to grumble and a major altercation seemed imminent. Suddenly Machiavelli approached.

"Peace, friends," Machiavelli urged, then whispered something in Mussolini's ear, whereupon Mussolini swaggered from the mirror and took his position at a distant tree. There, he folded his arms, and stuck out his chin and chest.

"What," asked Churchill in amazement, "did you say to him?"

"I told him," said Machiavelli, "that in a few minutes the line would form over there for the photographer."

Don't get stuck on your organization's image. You need to continually update it. Think of it as a Polaroid photograph that takes three years to fully develop.

As you take advantage of new opportunities, your vision should be flexible enough to accommodate them. Nonprofits tend to want permanence—to establish a path and stick to it forever. Alas, the world is in flux and you have to continually respond to its changing demands. So review and update your vision regularly. Every four to six months measure your performance against it. Are you delivering on your promise? Is the promise still accurate? Make adjustments. Then snap a new photo.

USE YOUR ENTERPRISE
TEAM TO...

1. Evaluate the results of your organizational questionnaire
2. Develop your lists of current and future operating characteristics
3. List your tangible and intangible assets
4. Divide your current audience into its many subgroups
5. Examine who else needs or wants the things your organization can do
6. Examine trends that may affect your markets and how you can capitalize on them
7. Brainstorm earned income ventures
8. Define where you want your organization to be in three years
9. Define your organization's area of specialty
10. Review the slogan and visuals that will communicate your vision to the public

PART IV

VENTURES:
MAKING THE FANTASY REAL

CHAPTER 18
WHAT IS A VENTURE?

Thomas Edison often remarked that the standard for his inventions was the silver dollar. "If it doesn't come up to that standard," said the great inventor, "then I know it's no good."

Part III of this book talked about developing an entrepreneurial vision for your organization. This section talks about turning that vision into profit-making ventures.

Ventures are projects that fulfill your mission and make money. They are distinct from "programs," which serve your mission, but do not necessarily make money. Some of your existing programs may be "repackagable" as moneymakers; others may continue to serve a valuable purpose in their current form. Hopefully, your new profit-making ventures will subsidize programs that don't pay for themselves. Your organization's catalog of activities will probably always include both types of projects.

CATEGORICALLY SPEAKING

Typically ventures fall into three categories: products, services, and special events.

PRODUCTS

Products are books, kits, videos, calendars, clothing, equipment...any tangible item you produce. However, unlike typical nonprofit products, which are sold retail to individuals, profit-making products are wholesaled to corporations for use as premium items. They can also be used as membership or fundraising incentives within your organization.

This British organization is well respected for its programs that assist sight-impaired people of all ages and incomes. While its services are valuable, it has struggled to appropriate enough funding for new programs. In recent years, RNIB wanted to establish a national helpline so citizens throughout the United Kingdom could contact the organization for local resources.

RNIB created a partnership with British Telecom (BT), a giant telecommunications company that is constantly on the lookout for new product markets. RNIB knew that one product sure to appeal to sight-impaired people—and virtually every aging person in Britain—was a big button phone! BT created the product, consulted with RNIB on marketing strategies that would appeal to targeted consumers, and launched a line of "In Touch" phones and accessories for individuals with various physical limitations. BT then promoted the message that approximately one dollar from every big button telephone sold or rented would go to RNIB and its new helpline program.

For RNIB, the joint venture has produced guaranteed cash and has introduced the organization to many other companies they might not have reached without the BT experience under their belts.

SERVICES

Most nonprofits are in the service business, yet few turn services into earned income ventures. Doing that is not difficult. Position your services as something that can be sold to corporations for use by their employees and customers.

Teaching, counseling, nursing—almost any service can work this way. Package an existing service for bulk corporate sale, or develop new ones. Be creative in thinking about what you have to offer. What skills exist in your organization that can become a service for corporate employees or customers? Here are some examples.

A nonprofit sports medicine clinic in the Midwest has been researching, diagnosing, and treating sports-related injuries for ten years. Patients come through referrals, advertising, and word of mouth. While business was good, it was unpredictable. The clinic had no way of knowing how many patients it would see each month, and how much income it would receive. The clinic wanted to expand its patient pool and stabilize its income.

To do this, it sold a package of services to the city school district. It now provides prevention education services to each junior and senior high school, and receives a monthly retainer to serve students who become injured during school sports. The contract not only stabilizes the clinic's income, it gives them access to an important audience. Their sports injury prevention message is being heard by a lot more people.

SAMPLE FILE

VANCOUVER
FAMILY
SERVICES

Vancouver Family Services does counseling for low- and middle-income people. Their clients come on a drop-in basis or through referrals from social service agencies. Most pay little or nothing. As a result, Vancouver Family Services was looking for ways to produce greater, more predictable income, and to reach new populations.

They have contracted with several local corporations to provide counseling services to employees. The corporations hire Vancouver Family Services on an annual retainer. The fee, based on the number of employees, covers a specified number of employee visits per year. If more employees seek the service, the corporation is billed for additional visits.

SPECIAL EVENTS

Special events put your organization in the public eye and reinforce your image and message. Even more important, they make guaranteed income before they take place (unlike traditional nonprofit promotional events, which provide goodwill but also create anxiety for the staff).

Special events are developed around a theme that relates to your mission, and include ways for corporations to participate. Whether through display booths, consultations, films, or seminars, businesses should be able to purchase time and/or space to communicate with your audience. Of course, their participation must be high quality and of value to your audience. Ordinary product ads and displays should be discouraged in favor of ones that teach important information. You want your audience to learn and enjoy—not to endure a sales pitch.

Help your business partners develop quality presentations and build that time into their fee. It's one more way you'll help them stand apart from their competition. Price each form of participation relative to its level of exposure. Sell as many of each form as you need to cover all costs of producing the event plus a profit. Charge an entry fee at the door, and keep those gate fees as profit.

Special events benefit from repetition. Whenever possible, make them annuals. Repetition strengthens the event's reputation, it builds expectations, and it enables you to capitalize on all you've learned in previous years. Staff, volunteers, and partners re-create the event with greater efficiency and profits improve.

Watch for signs of aging, however. Even the most popular events get tired, so keep them fresh by deleting and adding aspects. Then quit on a high. Four years is as long as most events sustain excitement with the public. Don't wait for yours to slide. Launch a new one. That will save you from overestimating income projections when the event starts to sag and will foster your image as a dynamic organization, always ready with something new. Allow nine months to a year to get a new event off the ground.

Time your special events to correspond with lows in your budget cycle. Special events provide chunks of cash, so use them to fill cash flow holes. But never do more than four events a year. Large events have a tendency to be disruptive no matter how well organized they are. One event per quarter is tolerable. More than that invites cries of mutiny.

What kinds of events can you do, and who could your sponsors be? Here is an example.

Colorado Academy is a private school in suburban Denver. They wanted to help parents find constructive summer activities for children and also wanted to generate income before the summer financial doldrums.

So the academy held a Summer Opportunities Fair. Summer camps, dude ranches, tour outfitters, sports facilities, and other summer activity providers bought booths and paid to place ads in the fair program book. It provided an excellent opportunity to reach their target audience.

But the school didn't stop there. They wanted the event to be free to families, so they developed three additional income sources. They sold a corporate partnership to Domino's Pizza. For a large fee, Domino's was listed in the program and had a booth at the fair. The academy rented food and drink concession stands and took a percentage of the sales. And they sold their mailing lists to the businesses that bought booths so those companies could have further contact with fair attendees. Fees paid by the business participants exceeded the costs of running the fair and Colorado Academy netted $10,000.

THEMES NATURAL TO US

Sometimes ventures group themselves naturally into themes. As you brainstorm possibilities, you may find products, services, and special events that serve the same audience or that relate to the same subject. Take advantage of it. Group those ventures into a package and give the package a name. Make it a major thrust of your enterprise strategy.

THEMES ADVANTAGEOUS

There are several advantages in creating a package of ventures.

- VENTURES CAN REINFORCE EACH OTHER. Having multiple ventures that appeal to the same audience or relate to the same theme enables you to say, "If you like our videotapes, you'll love our classes!" For-profits call this cross-promotion.

- VENTURE PACKAGES HELP DEFINE YOUR ORGANIZATION TO THE PUBLIC. If you can explain what you do in two or three large themes, your mission—and your vision—will be easily grasped.

- DEFINING PACKAGES MAY LEAD TO NEW VENTURES. Singling out an area of need or defining an area of activity may uncover additional products and services you can offer.

SAMPLE FILE

VANCOUVER YWCA

The Vancouver YWCA examined trends and found five expanded markets: working women, older women, women caring for older parents, women at home with young children, and single mothers. As they examined the needs of each market and the programs they could offer in response, the YWCA found the programs grouped into three areas: information and support, career development and leadership training, and increased services to their traditional audience, women in need. Setting the year 2000 as their goal for full program development, they created three packages, or initiatives:

INFORMATION 2000

Information 2000 positions the YWCA as the principal source of information for women, including publications, tapes, and classes with information on subjects from child care to fashion.

WOMEN 2000

Women 2000 is a leadership development program that will spawn networks between women in leadership roles and programs to help cultivate leadership skills.

SERVICE 2000

Service 2000 is a promise to deliver high-quality programs to low-income women, including a self-perpetuating endowment fund to support those programs.

The three initiatives support the YWCA's belief: "We help women cope and excel."

The Western Institute for the Deaf (WID) has a double mission. They provide counseling, interpretation, and job placement services to the hearing impaired, and handicap prevention and education services to the general public. As WID examined venture possibilities, they realized that all of their ideas focused on one of two goals: to popularize handicaps by removing stereotypes about the disabled, and to prevent handicaps by educating people about unsafe behaviors. So they naturally created two initiatives: Popularization and Prevention.

POPULARIZATION

Under the umbrella of popularization, they are creating a variety of products and services that teach the public about handicaps. A portable mall boutique sells disabled dolls and children's books, and a traveling exhibit uses participatory activities to teach about disabilities.

PREVENTION

Under the umbrella of prevention, WID markets products and services designed to help prevent hearing impairments. These include Hearing Stimulation Kits for infants, Sound Smart kits to help people recognize unhealthy practices such as overly loud stereos and work sites, and windshield screens with a "healthy ears" message.

CHAPTER 19
KNOW WHAT YOU WANT

It's time for school. Business school, if you will.

Before you can choose a venture that is appropriate for your organization, you need to know what corporations and consumers want. Why? Because this will help you know what you want. You need to know more about how people in the for-profit world think, and how they talk. You can stay true to yourself, true to your organization's mission, and true to your enterprise goals, but knowing the lay of the corporate land will help you immensely.

MARKETING

More than anything else, what can you learn from corporations? You need to know that to a majority of workers around the world, marketing is a way of life. Everything about your organization can and should be marketing driven. What does that mean? It means that you see marketing as a way of problem solving.

What marketing really means is that you develop different strategies for achieving the same goal, then you evaluate which strategy is likely to work best, and then you go for it. It isn't a mystery; marketing is a process that goes on every day in every part of any company. If you think about it, it is also a process that goes on in our personal lives. When you decide what to have for dinner, you're marketing: What's in the fridge? What will the kids eat? What did we have last night? Asking these questions helps you decide the best meal option and gives you the answers you'll need to overcome possible resistance to your decision.

COMPETITION

Second thing you need to know: Your organization is a product and, yes, you have competitors. Think back, have you ever known the trepidation caused by being categorized as offering a "duplication of services"? That kind of phrase doesn't scare the for-profit sector. It just means that your company will be getting busy proving that its product is better than that of the competition.

As a nonprofit pursuing enterprise, you'll sooner have a spring in your step when you recognize that you are, indeed, selling something. Your donors, alumni, and/or members are your customers, and you can—and will—effectively challenge your competitors, even if they're bigger than you. (Remember Avis's great tag line "We Try Harder"? Their competition inspired that company to tremendous profitability.)

KNOW YOUR MARKET

Here's another important lesson from the corporate world, the all-important eggroll on the combination plate of those first two realities: Define your market. Not only do you have to know your market and your competition, you have to locate your target market, appeal to it, and serve it well. Many nonprofits think that if they just put out a shingle, people will magically appear who want to buy what they're selling. Nope. Not gonna happen. You must decide exactly who you want as your customers, with darn good research to back up that decision. And then you have to fight to attract and keep those customers.

WHAT DO YOU WANT?

Perhaps the most valuable lesson to learn from the corporate world is this: you have to know what you want and have a realistic assessment of your ability to go out and get it. The number one complaint companies have of nonprofits that ask them to partner on ventures is a weak knowledge of and interest in the corporation's objectives. If you know what you want and you believe that a particular company is the means to get it, you'd better have done your homework—on yourself, on your product, and on your potential partner.

This is key: As a nonprofit ready to pursue ventures, you must do the work of knowing who you are, knowing your organizational limitations, and still believing passionately in your ability to bring something great to the marketplace.

And, as you'll see as you choose your venture, that kind of intelligent passion goes a long way.

CHAPTER 20
CHOOSING A VENTURE

June 10, 1975

The day the U.S. Army gave a whole new meaning to having a birthday blast. Picture this:

The New York Yankees are celebrating "Army Day" at Shea Stadium (where the team is playing while Yankee Stadium is being renovated). Two 75mm cannons stand in centerfield, facing the American flag. (Army brass have assured the team that the cannons' paraffin will flash harmlessly.)

You're ready for this, right?

As the crowd waits in anticipation, a battery from Fort Hamilton fires the first salute. An ear-splitting boom shakes the stadium, followed by one, two, three more blasts. Smoke fills the stadium. The crowd shimmies with earthquake vibrations. What's this? Glass shatters in the lofty Diamond Club.

Uh-oh. They've blown out more than candles. They've taken out three panels of centerfield fence and a fourth is on fire. This party's over.

Even Walter Cronkite can't resist commenting, "Army 21, Fence 0."[3]

You may want to start enterprise with a bang, but you also want to leave your fences standing. How do you begin? With which venture should you start?

LOOKING AND LEAPING

The most important thing is to have a plan. Make sure you have a clear idea of your overall goals and of how your venture will contribute. It should serve your mission, reinforce your public image, and relate to other ventures you will do.

Be equally clear about the venture's goals. Is its purpose to reach a certain audience? To convey a certain message? To make a lot of money? Most likely, it's all three. Is that achievable? Be realistic. Too often nonprofits take on ventures because they *want* to do them, only to find afterwards that they didn't meet their goals. Don't be surprised.

Occasionally you may decide to do a venture that doesn't make a lot of money. That's okay, but choose that consciously. Realize the opportunity cost of doing it. Make sure the other reasons justify the time. Make sure your next one brings in big bucks.

STRAIGHT AND NARROW

To choose a venture, narrow your list of possibilities to the three with the greatest potential. These are the ones that are simplest to do, that go straight to your strengths, that require skills you have in-house, that fit your mission and vision, and that require the least capital.

When you've got three top choices, test them a little further. You need to know if the assumed market really exists, how much it will pay, and how much it will cost to produce the venture. It's time for a common sense feasibility study. Grab your paper and pencil, and test your top three ideas against the following nine questions.

NINE CRITERIA FOR SELECTING A VENTURE

1. **RELATIVITY.** You don't have to be Einstein to calculate if the venture is related to your mission. It should be to go forward! Of all the criteria, this is the most important. It is important to your board, to your constituency, and most important, to those bureaucratic demons at the IRS or Revenue Canada. As long as your earned income ventures are mission related, your income will not be taxable. If you're unsure of whether something is related, consult a tax attorney who is familiar with nonprofit enterprise. You can choose to do an unrelated venture, but that's not the easiest first step.

2. **PROFITABILITY.** To determine a venture's profitability, you will need to do a pro forma. This is your "best guess" estimate of your venture's income and expenses. This pro forma doesn't have to be lengthy or complex. A few phone calls to people who are familiar with that type of project should give you most of the information you need.
   - **DIRECT COSTS.** First, look at your direct costs in producing the venture. Include labor, materials, transportation, equipment rental, special services, postage, photocopying, and any other expenses that may be incurred.
   - **INDIRECT COSTS.** Next, look at your indirect costs. These include administrative staff time, rent, utilities, insurance, telephone, and any

other costs that will accrue to your organization to support the development and operation of this venture.

- **MARKETS.** Look at your markets. Who will want to buy this venture? How much will they buy? How much will they pay? Once you have these basic figures on paper, juggle them. Look for as many ways as possible to lower your costs and raise your revenue.

- **VARIABLES IN PRODUCING A VENTURE.** There are many. For instance, who makes the product or delivers the service? Who distributes it? Who advertises it? What if you had a book printed in Hong Kong? What if you hired a fulfillment house to distribute it rather than hiring a staff person? What if you hired contract staff to deliver the service rather than using staff on payroll? Can your corporate partner advertise your product or service so you don't need to pay for advertising?

- **WHAT IFS.** If the venture seems profitable, do some market "what ifs?". What if paper costs rise and expenses increase twenty-five percent? What if half as many businesses buy the book? What if they'll only pay half the price? Develop best- and worst-case scenarios. In its worst case, will the venture still turn a profit?

- **EXPERT SECOND OPINIONS.** Have your industry experts look over your figures and challenge your assumptions. Ask them to be conservative: Most ventures fail because their planners underestimate expenses and overestimate sales.

- **FINANCIAL GOALS.** How much money do you want this venture to make? Don't just make a profit; make enough of a profit to justify your time and effort.

3. **CASH FLOW.** The cash for producing a venture should come from your corporate partners, not from you. However, some ventures take cash up front for mock-ups (samples) or to do research. Will this venture drain cash when you can't afford it? Will it produce cash when you need it? Pick a venture that matches your ability to finance it.

4. **IMAGE.** Every venture should deliberately build your public image. Will its character, audience, quality, and message project your organization the way you want to be seen?

5. **KNOW-HOW.** Do you know enough about this type of venture and this subject to do it well? (If you're going to speak to the Hispanic community,

In 1987, Braniff Airlines ran an ad campaign targeted to Hispanic communities on Spanish-language television and radio stations. Braniff attempted to woo customers by offering leather seats. The radio commercials told listeners to fly Braniff *en cuero,* which means "in leather." But a similar Spanish expression, *en cueros,* means "naked"—and the two phrases sound identical when spoken quickly.

As we all know, TV often has more impact, and sure enough, the TV version was an eye-opener, inviting readers to fly *en cuero* and *con tres pulgadas mas,* meaning "with three inches more." Presumably the airline was referring to extra leg room, but those viewers who thought the voice-over said *en cueros* received an entirely different message.

do you speak Spanish?) Are you comfortable with the venture's level of complexity? Who on your staff can manage it? Is knowledgeable, affordable outside help available?

6. OPPORTUNITY COSTS. Every decision to do a venture includes a choice *not* to do a different one. What revenue will you not make because you didn't do the other? Will this venture provide enough benefits to compensate? Have you maximized profitability on all other projects before starting a new one? Aim to do fewer ventures with bigger payoffs, rather than many projects with smaller return.

7. RESOURCES. Does this project make the best use of your staff, time, expertise, money, program strengths, image, and physical assets? Are the resources you'll put into it proportional to the outcome? Proportional to your organization's size?

8. LOVE. Do you love it? Do you really want to do it? Will your staff and board get behind it and support it? Your passion for the venture will be your greatest sales tool. Love means never having to say you're sorry.

9. DEMAND. You may have a great idea for a venture, but if you can't sell it, it's not worth much. How many businesses or individuals will want to buy it? How much will they buy? How much will they pay?

To answer these questions you need to measure the market. The research doesn't have to be extensive—or expensive. There are simple ways to gather the information. And of course, we're going to show you how. Turn the page.

CHAPTER 21
MARKET RESEARCH

Don't use research like a drunk uses a lamp post;
use it for illumination, not support.
—DAVID OGILVY, ADVERTISING KINGPIN

NOSEY PARKER'S FOOTSTEPS

During the early years of the first Queen Elizabeth's reign, Archbishop Matthew Parker of Canterbury found himself between church reformers and dogmatists in the bitter fight over church doctrine. To Parker the question was, "What do the people want and need?" So, step by step, he investigated specific issues rather than the larger rhetorical ones. (Not surprisingly, the origin of the word "investigate" comes from the Latin "follow a footprint.") Though risky, Parker's investigations led him to renounce Puritanism, to moderate church defections, to write the first privately printed English book, and to eventually earn him the label "Nosey Parker," a term than lives on today, more than four hundred years later.

It's time for you to pick up the scent. In doing market research, follow one footprint at a time. Do not ask questions beyond your reach. Start with manageable ones.

Then, will you know if people will buy your venture? You'll never know for sure until you actually do it. Enterprise is for people who are willing to take risks! But a little market research can take some of the anxiety out of the process, and can give you useful data for plugging into your pro forma.

FUNDAMENTAL QUESTIONS

The point of market research is to answer some fundamental questions: Is there an adequate market for the venture? How much will people pay? What's the competition? Will enough people buy yours to make the venture worth doing? Do the people understand what you are selling? Contrary to common belief, you don't need to hire a research firm, hold focus groups, talk to people in shopping malls, conduct telephone interviews, or spend a lot of money to find the answers. You do need to talk to people who *have* done those things.

And you can be sure someone has, no matter how arcane the data may seem. From the American Pencil Collectors Society and the National Pygmy Goat Association to the Flying Funeral Directors of America and the Desert Fishes Council, some group somewhere has collected the data you need. Your job is to find out when. Fortunately, your first step is small and easy to take. In just nine places you'll find most of the information you'll need.

RULE OF THUMB

KEEP RESEARCH EXPENSE IN PROPORTION TO YOUR INVESTMENT AND EXPECTED RETURN.

NINE EASY PLACES

1. THE INTERNET. No doubt about it. Here is your ultimate research tool. Do not limit yourself to one search engine; different engines often bring up radically different resources. The Internet is also a great way to access the following eight easy places, and to establish dialogues via e-mail with people working in particular fields.

2. INDUSTRY TRADE GROUPS. As with the pro forma, your most important source of information will be people who do this type of venture all of the time. They not only know costs and procedures, they know their markets. They will assist you with pricing, sales trends, consumer attitudes, competition, and other information that helps you gauge the market for your venture. Industry trade groups produce publications and compile research that is generally available for free. Use them to find experts in that field. People love talking about what they do; they will generally give you as much information as you want.

3. POPULAR MAGAZINES. If you want information on your target markets, read the magazines they read. Look at the issues that are discussed. Look at the products and services that are advertised. Ask the magazine to send you their readers' profiles. These will give you information about their ages, incomes, lifestyles, and buying habits. Run your idea past people in

the advertising and editorial departments; they sell to their readers all the time, and they know what they buy.

4. RESEARCH GROUPS, NATIONAL SOCIAL SERVICE AGENCIES, GOVERNMENT AGENCIES. If you are contemplating a venture that addresses a particular social need, consult an agency in that field. They will help you define the need, the market, and probable solutions. The local government and public library can help you find the right agency.

5. CHAMBERS OF COMMERCE. If you are planning to sell a venture to local business, consult the chamber of commerce. They know the local business scene. Chambers often have terrific Web sites that share specific information about their members.

6. BROKERAGE HOUSES. If you are considering a venture in a particular industry, or thinking of selling a venture to a company in that industry, go to a brokerage house that analyzes that field. They can give you industry costs, profits, and trends, and information on the companies you're considering approaching.

7. THE PUBLIC LIBRARY. Take the time to go to the business section of your public library. Some of its resources are better utilized in print formats, not via the Internet. Here, you will find a gold mine of information on individual companies and industries. You can find a particular company's advertising budget, staff size, vice presidents' names, and other information that will help you evaluate their buying potential (plus help you make sales contacts later). Particularly helpful are

• *The Standard Directory of Advertisers:* Also known as the Advertiser's Red Book, it lists companies doing national or regional advertising.

• *Standard and Poor's Register of Corporations, Directors and Executives:* Lists corporations and their offices, Standard Industrial Classification codes, annual sales, number of employees, subsidiaries, and more.

• *Dun and Bradstreet's Billion Dollar Directory:* Provides detailed marketing data about the top U.S. parent companies.

Make friends with the business librarian and have him or her show you the ones most useful to your venture.

8. BUSINESS MAGAZINES AND NEWSPAPERS. Reading business magazines and newspapers is vital for several reasons. They will help you stay on top of trends in the market; they'll give you ideas for new opportunities; they'll

reinforce your market orientation and enterprise attitudes. The business section of your local newspaper is equally important. Look for trends in the local community, businesses that are doing well and might be ripe for a venture, and stories about new or unusual executives who might be open to working with you.

9. LOVERS, FRIENDS, AND POTENTIAL USERS. When you've exhausted these resources, and you've winnowed your list of possible ventures to the two or three that seem most likely to succeed, do some informal data gathering among people whose opinions you respect. Start with people closest to you, the ones who want to keep you from humiliating yourself. Then move out to people who have known you for a long time and know your capabilities. Finally, talk to people who might actually buy your venture. Ask each person: Would you buy it? How much would you pay for it? How would you be better after using it? Ask people who you know will give you honest answers; they'll be your most valuable market research tools of all. Trust them.

Another word about market research. It won't buy you certainty. Nothing does. (Ironically, Matthew "Nosey" Parker was also chaplain to Anne Boleyn, whose passions led to too much research. She didn't know when to stop sampling.) Enterprise is for people who know when to stop juggling numbers and take a risk. Trust your gut; don't go beyond and lose your head.

RULE OF THUMB

NO AMOUNT OF RESEARCH WILL GUARANTEE SUCCESS.

CHAPTER 22
PRICING

You've heard the first rule of real estate, "location, location, location." Well, the first rule of sales is "price, price, price." It's great to develop and sell a product or service, but if you can't price it to make a profit, you might as well not do it.

Pricing is a poker game, a bluffing match. Every venture, every person has a price above or below which they won't go. We call that the "walk away price" or, in poker parlance, the "cattle" hand.

TEX LAGGARD

Tex Laggard was a cattle hand in the Old West. Like the other grizzled men of the sage and cactus, he was ready for the roundup. All the men were. 'Cept they had to share the cookin' while they were out on the range, and not a man in the group could cook a lick. It was hard being out there in the heat and dust. But what was hardest was the food. It was gawdawful. Still, no one dared complain; first man to say somethin' nasty about anyone else's cookin' had to cook for a week.

By the third week out Tex Laggard was gettin' ornery, he was starvin' for some decent food. As much as he hated to cook himself, he sure loved to eat. But he had a bad feelin' about what dinner'd be like tonight. Pug St. Claire was cookin' and Pug was the worst cook of the bunch.

When Tex sat down next to the other boys, not a one of 'em was eatin'. Everybody was starved just ten minutes before. They all just sat there lookin' at each other, the stew steamin' up out of their bowls, everyone sniffin' and kinda turnin' away, not sure.

Tex looked over at Pug St. Claire. The old buzzard had his back to the group. Tex couldn't tell if Pug was coughing or sneezing, but damn! Tex was hungry.

"Well come on, boys, ya gotta eat...," said Tex picking up his big old soup spoon. "Ya know the rules." He dove into it. All the men lurched forward. Even St. Claire glanced over his shoulder in surprise. There was a moment, nothing more, before Tex's eyes turned to pinpoints, then disbelief...."This tastes like cow patties!"

Every man gasped; St. Claire glowered.

Then Tex remembered how he hated to cook. "Tasty though."

Tex Laggard had his "walk away price," his "cattle" hand; no way was he going to cook for a week. That was his bottom line. You need to hold a cattle hand, too, every time you sidle up to the poker table of business partnerships.

YOUR CATTLE HAND

In your case, as an enterprising nonprofit, it's your costs. That's where you draw the line. You're going to need accurate accounting of direct and indirect costs:

- DIRECT COSTS are the labor, materials, printing, transportation, photocopying, and other "hard" expenses incurred by the venture.

- INDIRECT COSTS are the portion of your overhead that you can attribute to the venture: salaries, rent, utilities, insurance, etc. You can compute your indirect expenses based on actual time spent and space used, or you can apply a percentage of your budget. If you use a percentage, be sure it's high enough to adequately cover the costs.

Total your direct and indirect expenses and never sell a project for less! Never! In fact, don't sell a project for that price either, because you'll forfeit your profit. Add some profit to your costs and make that your walk away price. Tex Laggard and Pug St. Claire both had bottom lines. Your walk away price has got to be yours.

BLUFFING FOR FUN AND PROFIT

The easiest *and* safest way to price something is with "cost plus" pricing. That means you start with your costs and add on a profit to reach your sales price. Start by doubling your costs. That's called "keystoning." The one hundred percent keystoning markup covers your competence, credibility, and expertise. Many businesses price merchandise at "keystone plus twenty-five percent" or more, so don't be afraid of overpricing.

Typically nonprofits underprice. They fear if they price something too high, the corporation will permanently reject the deal. They won't! If a company is interested in a venture, they'll always listen to a lower offer. If you've started negotiating too low, however, you can never get the price back up.

RULE OF THUMB

"KEYSTONE" TO PRICE YOUR PRODUCTS AND SERVICES. DOUBLE YOUR COSTS TO CREATE YOUR PROFITS.

EXAMPLE:

	25 CENTS	(DIRECT EXPENSE)
+	25 CENTS	(INDIRECT EXPENSES)
+	50 CENTS	(KEYSTONE: 50 CENTS PROFIT)
=	$1.00	(SALES PRICE)

DON'T LOOK NOW, BUT IT'S THE BIG BOYS

Nonprofits are so used to small numbers, they forget the scope of a corporate budget. Businesses are used to paying large amounts for services and they value what they pay for. Make sure your price is one a company will take seriously.

For example, a small nonprofit that specializes in dispute resolution sold a package of services to a large corporation. Midway through the contract, the company's personnel manager, the man who had hired the organization, approached the nonprofit's director. "You know," he said, "you guys are doing great work. You've eliminated a lot of tension in our company, and I have to say, I'm surprised. I didn't think you'd be able to do it. I mean, I knew you'd do something good—but I didn't think it would be that good. Your fee was so low, I just didn't think we'd get that much for it."

With a corporate budget of close to a billion dollars, the personnel manager was used to spending hundreds of thousands of dollars a year on services for his employees. In his way of thinking, $16,000 (the fee charged by the nonprofit) couldn't buy enough time to produce a quality product.

WHINE COUNTRY

Your price should have enough of a sting for the company to feel your confidence and professionalism. They should say "ouch" before accepting it. They may whine about the price, but that's OK. It increases the value of the venture.

As an example, an enterprise consultant recently did a daylong seminar for a group of nonprofit organizations. The normal per person fee for such seminars is $125 per person, but a local bank had underwritten the opportunity and thus the cost came down to $30 per person. One hundred eleven people had prepaid and registered for the session, but when the consultant got to the hotel, a quarter of them had not come. He was surprised because generally his seminars play to full houses. "Oh, don't feel bad," his host assured him. "It's been raining here a lot and today is a beautiful day."

What she did not add was that at $30 people could "afford" to skip his seminar. At $125 they wouldn't have considered it and would have, instead, been at the hotel and ready to listen to what he had to say. There was not enough "ouch" in that price!

NEGOTIATING

Unfortunately, pricing is not always a matter of stating your price and then shaking on the deal. Frequently you have to negotiate. That's why, before you go into any sales meeting, you do your homework. There are some things to know to negotiate effectively.

- **KNOW WHAT THE MARKET WILL BEAR.** Talk to people in the advertising business and the business you plan to approach. Find out what corporations generally spend on this type of activity. Are there companies that provide similar services? What do they charge?

- **KNOW YOUR VARIABLES.** There's more than one way to produce your product or service. What can you add or subtract to change the price? If a four-color book is too expensive, sell them three colors. If your proposed oddball page size overshoots their budget, switch to a standard size. If small-group employee seminars strain their budget, offer one class for the whole team. The better you know your product and its options, the better deal you'll cut.

- **KNOW WHAT THE CORPORATION HAS TO SPEND.** You probably won't find out exactly, but by doing some snooping you can get a good idea. Nosey Parker lives! If it's a national company, look in The Standard Directory of Advertisers for the company's advertising budget and breakdown. That will tell you how much they allot for this type of venture annually. Get as much information from your contact as you can. Press gently but firmly.

- HOLD OFF ESTABLISHING A PRICE UNTIL AFTER YOUR FIRST SALES MEETING, IF POSSIBLE. Once you've got the corporation interested, they will be more open to negotiating price, and during your meetings you can extract information that will help you price the venture accurately. Here's an example of how this happens.

THROWING THE LAMB CHOP PAST THE WOLF

Jennifer Sawyer is director of enterprise at a senior center. The organization has an idea for a booklet called "In Celebration of Aging," a compendium of stories about men and women enjoying their later years. She is pitching the idea to the vice president of marketing at a retail drug store chain.

VP: Okay, what's it going to cost?

SAWYER: Well, first let's talk "what ifs." How are you going to use this book? Do you want a self-liquidating premium or a free one? Do you want people to pay a little bit for it, or do you want to give it away free?

VP: I think we have to go free with this one. We've tried self-liquidation in the past and they haven't worked so well. In fact one time—

SAWYER: —Alright, how many copies do you think you'll need? Give me a range—minimum, maximum.

VP: Uh, well, we're opening a new store in a couple of months in an area that's heavily populated with retirees. If we offer it as an opening giveaway—our gift to the community—we could probably use ten thousand. Yes, ten thousand would probably do it. Could we get more if we ran out?

SAWYER: We would own the copyright. You could buy more. But your second printing costs would drop. Of course, if you bought more the first time around, your per-unit cost would drop considerably.

VP: I suppose we could buy more, but I'm not sure what we'd do with them. I don't want to get stuck with a closetful.

SAWYER: Could you use them as a sales inducer in one of your other stores—give one away with every purchase over $10.00?

VP: Maybe. Actually, we could give them to our major suppliers too. If we did that, we'd probably need a hundred thousand.

SAWYER: Whoa! That really changes your price. On numbers like that you will definitely see your per-unit costs drop.

VP: That's true....Well, tell you what, give me a price on ten thousand, fifty thousand, and a hundred thousand. I'll have to go over this with our CEO, and that way we'll have enough information to make a decision.

SAWYER: How much do you generally spend on a premium like that?

VP: It depends. Sometimes the company buys them. Sometimes it's up to individual stores. When the company buys them we can spend more. Say up to 50 cents apiece. The individual stores won't spend that much. They usually won't go past 25 cents.

SAWYER: Well, 50 cents will buy you a slick, four-color piece, if the larger quantities hold. For 25 cents you're probably looking at something two-color, a little smaller. Fewer pages.

VP: I'm not promising anything, but we'll look at it both ways.

SAWYER: Your new store opens in March, so you'd want the booklets delivered by February 15?

VP: Yes, that'd be great.

SAWYER: Fine, I think I've got it. I'm going to get you prices on 10,000, 50,000, and 100,000 in two price ranges: under 25 cents and under 50 cents. Right?

VP: That should work.

SAWYER: Fine. I think we have made a good start. I'll get back to you in a few days with prices.

Through this exchange, Sawyer whet the vice president's appetite without letting him take a bite out of her meaty sales pitch. What's more, Sawyer gleaned a lot of information that will help her price the booklet in a range the company can afford. She's also picked up useful information on the company that will help her with later ventures. If there's one criticism, it's that Sawyer cut off the VP when he was about to reveal past problems with self-liquidators. Valuable information was lost because Ms. Sawyer wasn't listening. Overall, though, a good meeting.

Nonprofits tend to accept the first deal that's offered. They aren't used to wheeling and dealing. Often the first offer is not the best. If you've established a price for your venture that you know is competitive, don't give it away for much less. Tell the corporation you think you can do better. Talk to their competitors. If the corporation thought there was any merit in your venture, that alone may bring them back. If not, you may find a better deal next door. At any rate, never offer a product or service without a reasonable profit margin for your organization. It's not good business.

The Dairy Barn is a small arts center in Athens, Ohio. A few years ago, it came up with an unusual—and lucrative—idea for a special event that would give the center wide national recognition. The event was the National Jigsaw Puzzle Championships, a lively two-day contest in which jigsaw puzzlers from across the country would compete in the art and sport of puzzling.

The Dairy Barn sold the concept to Hallmark, makers of Springbok puzzles. For Hallmark the event was a natural. It gave them a chance to unveil their new line of puzzles. It gave them a chance to associate with a high quality institution, and it gave them tremendous national publicity. Over seven hundred puzzlers gathered to compete for the title of "world's fastest puzzler." Others submitted entries for new puzzle designs. The event was covered on *Good Morning America,* in *Sports Illustrated,* and in other media Hallmark could never have afforded to purchase. Clearly this was an event to repeat.

They did. The two partners went on to do the National Jigsaw Puzzle Championships for four years in a row. The fifth year, however, Hallmark changed the rules. Because of internal changes in the company, Hallmark's management wanted to rewrite the championship contract in a way that was less favorable to the Dairy Barn. Shrewdly, the Dairy Barn refused. They knew they had a hot item, and they decided to take it elsewhere. Their savvy paid off. They offered the championship to American Publishing Company, which bought it on the Dairy Barn's terms. The two new partners went on to do the event for another two years.

CHAPTER 23
FINDING CORPORATE PARTNERS

Familiarity, truly cultivated, can breed love.
—DR. JOYCE BROTHERS, PSYCHOLOGIST

Finding the right partner is not a chance affair. Patience, homework, and common sense will point you to companies likely to buy your venture. Be your own matchmaker. Look for companies whose markets, image, and interests match your own. The closer they match, the more likely a partnership.

DO THE SAME PEOPLE INTEREST YOU?

Remember, there are three fairly realistic stereotypes of the kinds of companies best suited to become your partners. Affinity corporations are those that have something in common with you. Defensive corporations need goodwill among their customers to combat bad PR or poor business performance. And opportunistic corporations are those who look at you and say, "Wow, this is a great chance for us!" (These, as you might have guessed, are usually our favorites.)

Match point #1: Look at the audience. ANY CORPORATION THAT WANTS TO REACH THE PEOPLE YOU SERVE IS A POSSIBLE PARTNER. Look at the buying habits of your markets. What do they buy? Who do they buy from? Those businesses can use your help to reach their customers.

SAMPLE FILE

SWIM B.C.

Swim B.C. is the provincial swimming association in British Columbia. Its goal is to interest people in the sport of swimming and train competitive swimmers. Al Heather, Swim B.C.'s executive director, read the book, *Mentally Tough,* which suggests that corporations use sports training techniques to hone their corporate competitive edge. Instantly he recognized a potential venture. He called Peter

McLaughlin, the book's author, and proposed a joint seminar for corporate executives.

Using techniques developed by Swim B.C., author McLaughlin would train executives in the principles of his book. The seminars, which would be held at Swim B.C., would be expensive and exclusive, and everybody would benefit. Executives were to learn valuable techniques, McLaughlin would publicize his book, and Swim B.C. would gain visibility and recognition. In the process, they would also meet corporate executives (all of whom would be potential venture partners) and they would make money. McLaughlin agreed.

The next challenge was to find a corporate partner. If the seminar was to make money, it needed to be organized as a special event. All costs would need to be covered up front. Money from seminar attendees would then be profit. What company would want to partner such an event? The answer was another question: What company wants to reach leading corporate executives in the United States and Canada? Well, there are many possibilities. Banks, brokerage firms, equipment manufacturers, and telephone companies, to name a few.

Al Heather approached several corporations, and after a few phone calls and meetings, Kodak Copier Division agreed to partner the seminar. Together, Kodak, Swim B.C., and McLaughlin developed the "Mentally Tough Seminar." It attracted 270 attendees and netted $10,000 for Swim B.C. The organization also strengthened its visibility and image, and favorably impressed 270 corporate executives with its ability to conceive and manage a business venture. Kodak, for its investment, reached that many potential business customers with a product and message they valued highly. Because of the success of the seminar, the three partners are now planning to take the event national.

INTRODUCTIONS BY RELATIVES

Match point #2: Look at the field of endeavor. ANY COMPANY IN A BUSINESS RELATED TO YOURS IS A POSSIBLE PARTNER. What companies make products or provide services that relate to your field or to the subject of your venture? Associating with you will increase their credibility with their customers.

SAMPLE FILE

DAIRY BARN AND SHOPSMITH

Remember the Dairy Barn, the small arts center in rural Ohio? They developed a second partnership with Shopsmith, manufacturer of power tools. When the Barn wanted to produce a traveling show on the art of woodworking, they needed underwriting for the costs. Enter Shopsmith. The show was perfect for their marketing needs. It associated their tools with the finest woodworking in the nation, and placed their name squarely before their target audience. In fact, Shopsmith not only underwrote the show, they advertised it. They enclosed entry forms in all their orders, putting word of the show in the hands of forty thousand woodworkers.

NOT-SO-BASHFUL ADMIRERS

Match point #3: Look for demonstrated interest. A COMPANY THAT HAS ALREADY DEMONSTRATED AN INTEREST IN YOUR ORGANIZATION'S AREA OF SPECIALIZATION is an obvious prospect. If they are already interested, you won't have to work hard to convince them. Working with you—an expert in the field—will better help them achieve their goals.

SAMPLE FILE

SMOKING POLICY INSTITUTE

When the Smoking Policy Institute wanted to build business, they designed a seminar for corporate personnel managers. The seminar would introduce managers to the problems of smoke in the workplace, and (parenthetically) suggest that the institute could solve them. But how to reach the managers? Easy. They went to Prudential Life

---

Insurance Company. Prudential had long encouraged business customers to implement health promotion programs. That positioned them as caring and lowered employee claims. Taking that reasoning one step further, the institute suggested that Prudential sponsor its smoking seminars around the country and invite its business customers to attend. Prudential agreed. They liked the opportunity to strengthen their caring message, and the institute got its message heard for free.

FAMILIAR LINES

MATCH POINT #4: Look for compatible marketing themes. A COMPANY WHOSE MARKETING THEME IS SIMILAR TO YOURS, OR SIMILAR TO THE THEME OF YOUR VENTURE, will be interested in what you have to offer. Your venture will give concrete form to the abstract values they espouse in their campaign, and will reinforce their campaign in the mind of the public.

SAMPLE FILE

SUSAN G. KOMEN BREAST CANCER FOUNDATION

One of the true powerhouse networks in nonprofit enterprise activity is the effort carried out by several organizations to find a cure for breast cancer. The Susan G. Komen Breast Cancer Foundation certainly does its homework. It does extensive research to identify corporations with marketing needs similar to their own and to link their cause to the consumers such corporations are aggressively targeting.

The foundation learned that Yoplait Yogurt was looking for a way to tell its primarily female customers that it cares about women's health concerns. Yoplait signed on and began producing bright pink lids for its cups of yogurt. During a specific period of time, consumers could forward these lids (clean ones, we hope) to Yoplait's parent company General Mills, which would donate 25 cents for each lid received to the Susan G. Komen Breast Cancer Foundation.

The "Save Lids to Save Lives" campaign has raised at least $100,000 for the foundation's research. The marketing program made real Yoplait's theme of meaningful concern for women's health issues and demonstrated their commitment to their customers.

The Giraffe Project is a national nonprofit that encourages people to "stick their necks out" to make a difference in society. Giraffe directors recognized a natural partner when they saw an ad in the newspaper for a large insurance company. The company's campaign slogan was "Everyone can make a difference." What a perfect match for the Giraffes!

They quickly put together a package of ventures that would meet both parties' needs. The two organizations have negotiated the series of ventures. We'll tell you more about them in Chapter 25. They will provide benefits to the company's employees. They will reinforce the company's slogan. They will spread the Giraffe's message and earn income for the project.

LOOKING FOR MR. DO-GOOD

Okay, so you're ready to get familiar with potential partners. How do you find companies that match your interests and audiences? By using the same techniques and resources you used for market research.

- MAKE A HABIT OF READING BUSINESS PUBLICATIONS. THEY WILL HELP YOU UNDERSTAND HOW BUSINESSES THINK AND WHAT THEY'RE LOOKING FOR. *The Wall Street Journal, Advertising Age, Fortune,* and *Inc.* are good resources, as are *Corporate Philanthropy Report* and *Causes and Effects,* publications that document partnerships between the for-profit and nonprofit sectors.

- LOOK FOR FEATURE STORIES ABOUT UNUSUAL COMPANIES AND EXECUTIVES. Those that are singled out for interesting reasons may be more open-minded, more savvy, and better prospects for unusual ventures.

- **LOOK FOR ADVERTISING SLOGANS THAT PUT A PREMIUM ON VALUES.** Words like "excellence," "leadership," and "achievement," which mesh with your own intangibles, can give you a hook to hang a venture on.

- **CALL THE MARKETING DEPARTMENT.** When you find an ad that suggests its company is a likely partner, call their marketing department. Find the person who approved the ad. Tell him or her why you like their ad (people love compliments) and why your organization is a good match with theirs. Don't call the ad agency. Agencies have a way of forgetting or distorting ideas that aren't their own. What's more, they have no bottom line reason for passing your ideas onto their client.

- **LOOK AT COMPANIES THAT ARE ACKNOWLEDGED FOR THEIR VALUES.** *100 Best Companies to Work for in America and Canada* and *America's Corporate-Conscience* are books that list companies that take pride in the same values you do. They may be likely partners.

- **CHECK EXISTING RESEARCH ON CORPORATIONS.** You can find information about companies you're interested in by studying existing research generated by the United Way, chambers of commerce, banks, brokerage houses, industry associations, and magazines. Often they'll let you use it for free.

- **GO TO A COMPANY THAT HOLDS SECOND POSITION IN ITS FIELD WHENEVER POSSIBLE.** They need to work hard to catch up; they may be more willing to try the unusual.

FINAL PREPARATIONS

Once you've reduced the field of possible partners to two or three, do a little more homework. Gather as much information about those companies as possible. Consult each company's Web site and check out the links it has set up to other sites. Also read the Web sites of their strongest competitors. Even if those companies are not potential partners, this will help you understand the competitive mind-set of the companies you plan to target. Read each corporation's annual report. Find out their advertising budgets and the breakdowns of how those budgets are spent. That will give you an idea of how much money they might have to spend on your venture. Get the names of CEOs and marketing executives so you know whom to contact.

Look at their past advertising campaigns and products. Does your venture jibe with things they've done before? Talk to people who know the companies, to gather as much information as you can. All this data will help you structure ventures to best meet each company's needs.

The more you read, the more you talk to people, the more in touch you are with the business world, the easier it will be to spot potential partners and get familiar with them. Like everything else in enterprise, it's a matter of attitude. Once you start thinking like a businessperson, you'll start attracting partners.

Of course, business partnerships are like any other; they're based on mutual satisfaction. As soon as one partner is unhappy, the relationship generally ends. So keep in touch with your partners' needs and keep them mindful of yours.

CHECKLIST: CORPORATE VENTURE GUIDELINES

As you design your ventures, think about them from your potential partner's point of view. Keep asking yourself: Will this meet several of the company's needs? Will it be easy to implement? Will it work for their audience?

Payless Cashways, a national home building supply chain, expects the following qualities in a joint venture with a nonprofit. Keep them in mind as you develop your own ventures. They will give you a good idea of what your potential corporate partners will be looking for.

1. The theme of the venture should
   - Be "warm and fuzzy" and appeal to customers' altruism
   - Be simple, distinctive, and easy to grasp
   - Appeal to as wide an audience as possible
   - Promote our marketing message
   - Strengthen our image as good public citizens
   - Be related to our line of business, if possible

2. The venture should promote sales and/or build traffic to our business.

3. The venture should appeal to employees. It should offer them a way to be involved and, if possible, control elements of it.

4. The venture should be easy to operate. It should be managed by the nonprofit (or an outside contractor) and should require little time from corporate staff.

5. If the venture starts locally, it should have regional and/or national rollout potential.

6. The venture should be easy to explain and defend to shareholders.

7. The venture should be newsworthy and appealing to the media.

8. The venture should be compatible with our corporate giving guidelines.

9. The venture should be low risk.

10. The venture could have a seasonal focus.

11. We should have exclusive rights to the program.

12. The venture should encourage the nonprofit's members and users to participate.

13. The structure of the venture should allow for corporate review at predetermined checkpoints.

CHAPTER 24
BRANDING IS EVERYTHING

*Well, listen here, pardner. You can't tell me that them cows in
that thar pasture are yours. You just take a look. You'll see that
every darn one of 'em has the double lazy bar circle Q on his behind
and that means they're MINE.*

You've done your homework. You have a good sense of companies to contact that will be interested in your venture idea. You've shamelessly introduced yourself to them using every trick in the book (yup, every trick in *this* book). Now, before you go any farther, you've got to stop in your tracks and take a good hard look at what's on your behind.

We're talking brand, pardner. When others look at you, what do they see? And what do they think of you because of it?

Be assured, any corporation you are approaching has thought about branding. They think constantly about what their customers think of them and why. Every one of their marketing strategies is designed to enhance a brand image because that's what people buy: They buy a name and a reputation every time they plunk down cash for a product or service.

The most successful stories of branding come from names that have become part of our vernacular. Stuffy nose? Here's a Kleenex. Need to send a letter by overnight mail? Fed Ex it. Even if you don't use that particular company when buying what you need, you often use a brand name to talk generically about a product or service.

As you start down the road of preparing your idea for sale, it is important for you to look at your brand. Are you well known in your community? Is your reputation a good one? Then you have a brand image that many corporations will want to associate themselves with.

Are you a young organization that struggles to get anyone to remember your name? If you are, then you know that "brand identity" is a valuable commodity. The Soho Repertory Theater in New York is a good example. This small organization needed to become better known for presenting provocative plays. One of its board members was a former marketing executive at the master of corporate branding strategy, Proctor & Gamble. He suggested to the artistic director that the theater staff analyze everything from the logo, to its presence in promotional efforts (such as in New York City cultural referral sites on the Internet), to the demographics of the theater's customer base, in order to develop a bold and consistent strategy for promoting Soho Rep. This is how a brand is born.

Corporations that respect the brand of a nonprofit organization will pay to associate with it. They still want to know about your venture partnership proposition, but your realistic assessment of your brand will carry a lot of weight in negotiations.

Having an established, positive brand identity is like having equity in a house. You own it, and it is a valuable asset. Don't underestimate its value, either.

If you recognize that you have brand equity, use it. If you think you are too young, too specialized, or too whatever, do not despair. Here's a quick guide to building your brand:

AT THE ORGANIZATIONAL LEVEL:

- What does your name say about you? Should it change (even slightly)?

- Do you have a slogan? Is it useful if associated with a corporation's goals? (For example, if your slogan is "making a difference for greater Milwaukee," there are dozens, if not hundreds, of corporations that could benefit from putting that phrase on their advertising or packaging.)

- Does everyone at your organization know what you do, where you came from, and who you serve? If they don't, start an education campaign immediately to make sure everyone—including the temp at the front desk—is on the same page, using the same words to communicate the same message.

AT THE GRAPHIC LEVEL:

- What does your logo look like? Is it still fresh? Where is it used and why? Investing in quality graphic design for a memorable logo can be worth a great deal of money when a corporate partner sees benefit in adding it to its promotional materials.

- What colors represent your organization? Think about this. We're not trying to be cute. If you like your colors and believe they communicate strength and purpose, then make sure everyone in the organization always uses exactly the same colors and color combinations.

- Every corporation has what are called "graphic standards." Every nonprofit should have them as well. These are the laws for how your image will and will not be used, and who has the authority to decide when and where your logo and name will be placed.

DETERMINE YOUR BRAND PERSONALITY:

- Decide what kind of emotional reaction you want your organization to generate. Make sure all your materials are consistent with that goal.

- List the character traits you want to be known for.

- Describe the words that you want to use to talk about yourself.

- Decide what really matters to you: Do you want to be bold and sassy or staid and respectable? Then choose everything from paper stock to typeface to communicate that personality style.

PLAN FOR FUTURE PRODUCTS AND PROGRAMS:

- Develop a plan for naming new ventures as well as new activities in the program area of your organization. Words matter. Simple, easy-to-understand names are critical.

- Always associate new products and programs directly with your organization's name. Don't let customers forget who "owns" that idea. When customers remember, potential corporate partners will remember as well.

Stealing the cows in the pasture over the hill isn't worth the effort when you know they are easily traced to their rightful owner. When your branding is strong and effective, your competitors will steer clear of the good qualities, images, and language you have cultivated to be associated with you and your products, and *only* you and your products.

CHAPTER 25
STRUCTURING VENTURES FOR SALE

Found on the grounds of a Japanese amusement park: musical bath slippers; a fig tree that dances to the music of Karen Carpenter; and a display of underwear with three leg holes. The garment is supposed to last for six days, with the wearer rotating it 120 degrees each day—and then wearing it inside out for three days.
—THE WALL STREET JOURNAL, OCT. 16, 1987

THREE LEGS UP

We all love choices, even if those choices sometimes seem a tad unbelievable. Cookie dough ice cream and the Palm Pilot turned out to be legitimate favorites, right? So it's not surprising that on the way to market, the successful entrepreneur offers his partners choice too, to insure their support.

When advertising executives sell corporate clients on a new campaign, they don't present just one option. They go in with a number of ideas because they know their clients like to choose. Selling a venture is no different.

Choosing makes people feel smart and in control. So when you propose ventures to a potential partner, don't offer just one option, offer three. But no more. They'll enjoy picking the one that's right for them, and you'll increase your chances of success. At least one of your three options is likely to be on target for meeting their needs, interests, and budget.

TERMS OF ENDEARMENT

Your three options should include ventures at different price points, so they can pick the price that fits their budget; and ventures with a range of complexity, so they can choose their level of time, effort, and involvement. Make some options "turnkey," that is, requiring no effort on the part of the company. Make others more interactive, giving company employees, distributors, suppliers, or even customers, a chance to be involved. If possible, offer ventures that meet both internal and external needs: something that benefits the corporation's employees, as well as something that boosts its image with customers.

You will also strengthen your proposal if you can offer the company a mini-marketing campaign rather than a list of isolated options. That means offering a logical series of ventures that take place in succession. Each one reinforces the others and reminds the public about the corporation's partnership with you. By building an ongoing relationship this way, you become an integral part of their marketing strategy. The longer the campaign lasts, the stronger your relationship will be, the more interest the corporation will have in insuring its success, and the more likely they'll want to repeat it.

SAMPLE FILE

GIRAFFE PROJECT

Remember the proposed project between the Giraffe Project and the insurance company? It is actually a series of ventures that form an ongoing campaign tied to the company's marketing theme. With the following package of options, the Giraffes meet their own goals of encouraging giraffe-like behavior, and help the company substantiate its slogan, "Everyone can make a difference."

1. *The National Giraffe Award.* Annually the insurance company would recognize a small number of people who had stuck their necks out and made a difference in their communities. The award would be administered by the Giraffe Project, for a fee.

2. *Giraffes: The Book.* The joint publication of a book chron icling inspiring stories of "giraffes." The book would be tangible proof of the company's commitment to its theme, and would provide a profit to the Giraffe Project.

3. *The Giraffe insurance premium check-off.* To reinforce its commitment to making a difference, the company would give one dollar to the Giraffe Project each time a subscriber checked this box on his premium.

4. *The Giraffe Contest.* In this special event organized through schools, children would be invited to write

stories about courage and community service. Winners would receive scholarships from the company. The Giraffe Project would receive a fee for administering the contest.

5. *Corporate Giraffe Award.* Annually, the company would recognize a small number of corporations for promoting giraffe-like behavior among employees and in their communities. The award would position the company as the exemplar of courage and community service. They would pay the Giraffe Project a fee for managing the project.

6. To promote well-being among company employees, the Giraffe Project also proposed:

    - *Internal Giraffe Award.* Annually the company would recognize employee-nominated internal "giraffes."

    - *Giraffe Project memberships.* For corporate employees and customers, purchased wholesale from the project for use as a premium item.

    - *A Giraffe Service Package.* For employees, this includes employee seminars on developing giraffe-like behavior; a children's growth chart that enables families to measure moral as well as physical growth; and a kit of family activities that encourage giraffe-like behavior.

OPPORTUNITY KNOCKS AND KNOCKS AND KNOCKS...

Another thing to keep in mind when structuring a venture is to maximize its income opportunities. Sell each venture many ways to many partners, and try to build multiple income streams into each one.

The Dallas Children's Theater produces an annual Family Arts Calendar, which provides six sources of income:

1. The group charges $3,000 for a full-page ad. Nine months x $3,000 generates $27,000 a year.

2. For $250 a performing arts group can have its performances listed on the calendar.

3. For $500 a group can include a discount coupon on the calendar's coupon page.

4. If a patron goes to any five performing arts performances during the year and sends in the ticket stubs, the Dallas Children's Theater sends him or her a free ticket to one of its own performances. Since most people go to the theater with someone, the free ticket usually generates additional paid ticket sales.

5. The calendar is sold in local stores for $6.50.

6. The calendar is also presold at bulk discount to PTAs, which sell it at full price and keep the difference. This strategy "mass baptizes" a huge sales force for the calendar, increasing its circulation and winning friends for the theater.

We mentioned that the Smoking Policy Institute sells videotapes and workbooks to a health insurance company as a premium item for business customers. But that is just one way the institute makes money from those materials. They have developed four additional income streams as well.

1. *Presales.* The materials were initially developed in an arrangement with Simon and Schuster. BBP, a division of Simon and Schuster, gave the institute an advance to create the tapes and books, and published them. The institute receives a royalty on every sale.

2. *Wholesales to nonprofits.* The institute wholesales the materials to nonprofit organizations in anti—smoking-related fields. The Canadian Cancer Society, for example, buys the materials at discount, then resells them to its own clients.

3. *Wholesales to for-profits.* The institute wholesales the materials to for-profit companies, including a smoking cessation company and a manufacturer of hospital equipment, who then resell the materials to their clients.

4. *Retail.* The institute retails the materials from its office, through brochures and customer contacts.

Through all of these arrangements, the SPI makes many more sales than it could ever make on its own.

CHAPTER 26
NO-RISK SALES

New Jersey is not all belching smokestacks and mobsters, but this is the caricature that often follows that state around. Perhaps that's why the civic-minded New Jersey Division of Gaming Enforcement (DGE) decided to take a no-risk approach to their work. In 1980 the DGE released its official report concerning local organized crime. The words "mob," "syndicate," "Mafia," and "Cosa Nostra" were completely avoided, and instead were replaced with "member of a career offender cartel." No risk, no pain.

IF IT'S YOURS, HOLD ON TO IT

We're talking money! And as we've said before, don't use your money, use theirs. Almost all nonprofit ventures can be accomplished with corporate money. Don't plan the event, don't write the book, don't build the exhibit, don't spend a dime (except on putting together your proposal) until you have sold it to a corporation. That way there's no cash outlay, no unsold inventory blocking hallways, and no risk to you.

Feel like the New Jersey DGE? Sound too good to be true? It's not. Corporations will use your product or service as a premium item. That means they'll distribute it (free or for a charge) to their customers or employees. They purchase premium items all the time. Why not from you?

YOUR THING IS THEIR THING

Here's how it works. You presell the product or service to the corporation. That means before the product is made or the service performed you sell a bulk number of units at a wholesale price. The price includes all your direct and indirect costs of producing the product, plus a profit. Because you have presold it, you are able to customize it for the corporation. If it's a book, you put their name on the cover or invite them to put a message from the president inside. If it's a service, you tailor it to their needs and you hold it at their sites. Once the deal is made, you produce the product or service at no risk or cost to you.

Imagine you're a literacy organization. You have an idea for a publication—a parent's guide to helping kids with homework. Who would want such a book? Any business that wants to reach families with a "we care about education" message. That's a long list: private day care chains, bookstores, school systems, children's clothing manufacturers, or any retailer or manufacturer selling primarily to families. The next question is: How to sell it?

THEIR THING CAN BE SOMEONE ELSE'S THING

PRESELL EXCLUSIVE RIGHTS TO A SINGLE CORPORATION. In doing research you may find that a major bookstore chain is launching a literacy campaign. Perfect! You offer them exclusive rights to your publication. They advance-purchase one hundred thousand copies at a price that covers all your direct and indirect costs plus a profit. You produce the book, put their name on it, and agree not to sell the book to any other partner, in any industry, anywhere in the world, at any time. This is frequently the best way to presell something because you can charge a premium price for exclusivity.

PRESELL TO CORPORATIONS EXCLUSIVE RIGHTS WITHIN THEIR INDUSTRY. Instead of selling the book to just one sponsor, you opt for multiple sales. You know a private preschool chain is opening new centers in your city and needs an enrollment incentive. A local department store is planning a large back-to-school promotion and would like a sales incentive. A local hospital is promoting its improved pediatric unit and could use a take-home reminder of its new services. You offer each of them exclusive use of the book within their field. They pay you to produce the book; they purchase advance copies. In exchange you promise not to sell it to any other preschools, department stores, or hospitals.

PRESELL TO CORPORATIONS FOR PRIORITY USE WITHIN THEIR INDUSTRY. Two toy manufacturers are promoting new lines of educational toys. Both might be interested in using the book as a premium, so offer one company use of the book for a limited time. They pay you to produce it and purchase copies in advance. For the specified time, they have exclusive rights to the book within their field. (You're free to sell it to a company in another industry.) When the time period expires, you presell the book to the second toy company.

PRESELL IT TO NONPROFIT ORGANIZATIONS. The local school district is a natural for your book. Presell to the district or the PTA. If they have trouble with the price, get a local bank or retailer to subsidize the purchase. They'll get two nonprofits for the price of one!

SELL IT TO A COMMERCIAL DISTRIBUTOR. You can't find a corporation or nonprofit willing to buy your book, so you go to a publishing house. They agree to publish it. Great for your ego, but bad for your bottom line. Because they take all the risk, you get a tiny percentage of the profits. Make this a last resort.

USE THE PRODUCT OR SERVICE YOURSELF. Regardless of what arrangements you make with corporations, negotiate your own use of the product. Use it as a membership premium ("Join at the $50 level and get..."), as a membership inducement ("Join now and get..."), or as a renewal incentive. Always try to use a product or service multiple ways.

PRESELLING DOS AND DON'TS

- Do increase the price—When you offer a corporation exclusivity, increase the price of the product or service to make up for "lost" sales to other businesses.

- Do presell as many units as possible—If you are selling a product, presell as many units as possible because the more produced, the lower the cost per unit. That increases your profit margin (or permits you to pass on a lower cost to each buyer).

- Do not become the distributor—We will say it again, do not become the distributor of your product. Have it shipped from the manufacturer to the corporation (or to their designated fulfillment house) or you are likely to lose the profit you just negotiated!

RULE OF THUMB

MONEY—DON'T USE YOURS, USE THEIRS.

CHAPTER 27
THE SALES CALL

My shoes have never done this kind of thing before,
They would not go out in the rain;
It was not me who tracked that mud across the floor,
I don't know how I can explain;
For years my shoes have been my friends,
I've taken them around the world and to its ends
Now they're taking me . . .
My shoes are
On top of the world,
My shoes are.
—THE BOBS, "MY SHOES"[4]

GIVING YOUR SHOES DIRECTION

You've got three great ideas, all reasonably priced, and a company you know will love them. How do you get your shoes in the corporate door? Once you're in, how do you get the company to pay attention? Don't let this sales stuff throw you. Corporate execs wear shoes just like you; you're already part of the club.

There are a variety of routes into a corporation, and whichever one you pick, your path to the right person may be circuitous. What you're proposing is new. The corporation may have done very little of this kind of marketing before so it will be hard for them to know where to begin. It may take three or four phone calls, or even meetings, to get the right party. Don't worry, your shoes are patient soles. Plus, it won't hurt for other players to hear the idea along the way. If your venture goes, it may involve them, too. Each contact strengthens your image as an imaginative, entrepreneurial nonprofit.

CALL SOMEONE WHO WEARS SHOES

If possible, start with a contact in the company. If you know the CEO, then by all means start there! If you've received donations, ask the contributions officer to direct you. If you've got a product or service for employees, call the vice president of employee relations. If you're approaching the company completely "cold," start with the marketing department. Someone in there must wear shoes. Even with marketing you have options. Pumps, oxfords? Who are the high heels? Should you call the vice president for marketing? For advertising? For public relations? Public affairs? Each of these people presides over a different aspect of the company's marketing pursuits—and they all wear shoes! The people in marketing and advertising usually have more clout than those in public relations and public (or community) affairs, but the latter may be the most initially receptive. Everyone has some affinity for shoes, so don't worry about getting tongue-tied: You belong.

RULE OF THUMB

TO A CORPORATION, YOUR BEST SELLING POINTS ARE THAT YOUR JOINT VENTURE IS AFFORDABLE, COMPETITIVELY PRICED, AND EXCLUSIVELY THEIRS.

BEFORE YOU GET THE BOOT

Wherever you start, the first thing you'll need to do is make clear that you're not asking for a contribution. Corporate managers are used to talking to nonprofits about handouts, not about business deals. It may take them a while to understand that you're proposing a joint venture that will meet *their* needs. Even when they get it, they may be leery of you because nonprofits are often unsophisticated in their approach to marketing, and bear an image of being antibusiness. You'll need to defeat those expectations. Remind them constantly that you mean business. Talk in their language. Avoid the jargon of your field.

When you get the marketing VP on the phone, tell them that you have a business proposition that will make them money. Be specific, tell them you'd like fifteen minutes next Tuesday to talk about it. Know that you are offering the VP your organization's valuable name, image, and experience. Know that your shoes support you every step of the way.

RULE OF THUMB

IF YOU CAN'T EXPLAIN YOUR CONCEPT
QUICKLY AND WITH ENTHUSIASM, FORGET IT.

NO LOAFERS ALLOWED

Once your shoes are through the door, challenge yourself to be even more businesslike than the people you're meeting. Tell them that you know they're busy, that they don't have much time. Remind them you said you'd take just fifteen minutes, and put your watch on the table to stress that. You tell them when the time is up. That puts you in control and impresses them with your ability to deliver.

Remember, as you talk, that these people are not philanthropists. They are not there to meet your needs, but rather to make money for their company. They're entering the meeting with five questions in mind, and you need to satisfy each of them before they will buy your venture. They want to know:

- WHAT'S NEW ABOUT THIS IDEA? "New" marketing ideas are a dime a dozen. What's new about this one? Why should we get excited?

- SO WHAT? It might be a good idea, but why should we want it? How will it benefit us?

- WHO CARES? Why will the public pay attention? Who will want it?

- DOESN'T SO AND SO DO THAT? Didn't our competition already do something similar?

- WHO ARE YOU? It's a great idea. We can see it will benefit us. But why should we trust you to pull it off?

You want to answer those five questions before they're even asked. Here's an example of how they might work.

All Ears is a hypothetical organization that provides counseling, education, and therapy for the hearing impaired. It has recently expanded its mission to include education for the general public to prevent unnecessary hearing impairments. With that goal in mind, Bill Schmidt, the organization's director, called the vice president of marketing at the largest local employer. Bill wants him to sponsor All Ears' mobile audiology clinic at his plant and in a local mall. The VP liked the idea over the phone, arranged a meeting, and asked the company's vice president for employee relations to sit in.

SCHMIDT: Tell me if I'm right, you want to demonstrate to this community that ABC Box Corporation is a genuinely caring and generous public citizen. And you want to demonstrate to your employees that you're concerned about their welfare.

VP/MARKETING: Well, of course.

SCHMIDT: I've got three products that will help you do it. They're all affordable, competitively priced, and would be exclusively yours. The first one is a turnkey operation. We'd like to bring our mobile audiology clinic to your plant and provide free hearing exams for ABC employees and their families. And we'd like to take it to Southgate Mall for four days during their back-to-school sale to do the same thing. Your name will go on the van. Interested?

VP/MARKETING: Tell me more.

SCHMIDT: First let me tell you a little bit about our organization. Then I'll describe the clinic and how it will meet your needs. All Ears is one of the most respected hearing health organizations in the country. You may already be aware that we've been serving the hearing impaired of Smith County for nine years, and we just won the Audiology Associates Award for excellence in our field.

VP/MARKETING: Mmm.

SCHMIDT: We serve approximately 26,000 people a year with a wide range of services, including hearing screenings, therapy, equipment prescription, counseling for the hearing impaired and their families, and education for the general public to prevent unnecessary hearing loss. We are a sophisticated organization with a staff of six and an annual budget of $160,000.

VP/EMPLOYEE RELATIONS: What does all this have to do with us?

SCHMIDT: We've recently begun selling a variety of products and services to diversify our income. The mobile clinic is one of our new services. It's housed in a self-contained fifteen-foot trailer that will park in your parking lot. It's staffed with three professional audiologists who can handle up to fifty people an hour. They'll do routine hearing tests as well as mini counseling sessions for people who have questions or concerns about their hearing. If the van operates from 8 A.M. to 8 P.M. Thursday through Sunday, we can screen approximately 2,400 people, or all of your workforce plus family members. We can also schedule longer appointments for people who would like them. The normal fee for this is $10, but your employees would get it for free, courtesy of ABC Box.

[The intercom buzzes. Frank, the VP's secretary, wants to know if VP can take call.]

VP/MARKETING: Tell him I'll call him back.

[VP looks back to Schmidt.]

SCHMIDT: We'll also take the clinic to Southgate Mall for four days in late August. The clinic will park at the main entrance to the mall. A large banner will say "All Ears Mobile Audiology Clinic brought to you by ABC Box Corporation." Newspaper ads and signs throughout the mall will advertise the clinic's presence and that it's available through your company's generosity. Approximately fourteen thousand people visit Southgate during the last weekend in August. It's their second busiest business time after Christmas, and mall managers estimate the clinic's presence can increase attendance by fifteen percent.

VP/MARKETING: Seventeen thousand people in eight days...that's an impressive number for a personal contact.

SCHMIDT: It also reinforces your corporate message that you are concerned about the health and education of your employees and your community. The clinic really makes tangible the promise you make in your ads when you say, "We care."

VP/EMPLOYEE RELATIONS: You're right about that. But don't the schools do this? Seems to me my kids get their ears tested in school every year.

SCHMIDT: Young children get their ears tested in school, but when was the last time you had your ears tested? Schools do a fine job with children up through second grade. After that, most people don't have their ears checked again until there's a problem. Then it's too late. Even when people do have their ears checked—whether it's in school or at the doctor's—they usually receive little education about preventing hearing loss. That's a large part of what the mobile clinic does. We tell people how to develop healthy hearing habits at home and at work. We'll send everyone home with a Hearing Habit Handbook—with ABC Box Corporation's name on it—to remind them how to keep their ears healthy for the rest of their lives. That's seventeen thousand in-home reminders about how ABC Corporation really cares about their health.

VP/EMPLOYEE RELATIONS: Hmm.

SCHMIDT: Well?

VP/MARKETING: I'm not sold. I think deafness is gloomy. I don't think people want to have their hearing checked. It's not sexy.

SCHMIDT: *Health* is sexy, one. And, two, people love learning about themselves. Have you ever seen anyone pass up a chance to learn something about themselves? Most people can't pass up a bathroom scale, even when they know they won't like what it says!

VP/EMPLOYEE RELATIONS: Ha! You've got a point there. But let me ask you a question. We've got a plant down in Springfield. Can we take it down there?

SCHMIDT: No problem.

VP/MARKETING: And can we do the mall there, too?

SCHMIDT: You bet.

[Schmidt knows the VPs are hooked, but VP/Employee Relations has paused.]

VP/EMPLOYEE RELATIONS: One last question.

SCHMIDT: Yes?

VP/EMPLOYEE RELATIONS: Where'd you get those shoes?

Schmidt's got them hooked, all right. There's a moment in a successful sales meeting when the corporate contact starts saying "we." At that moment he's bought into the venture. That doesn't mean your work is over. There are usually further sales to be made, to his boss, his boss's boss, maybe even to a marketing committee. However, from that point on, your contact will be your ally in selling to the rest of the company. Checking their feet, you're bound to notice...they all wear shoes. Members of your club!

TOEING THE MARK

Up until that point, you purposefully haven't talked price. Always get them excited about the idea first—make them want it—then tell them what it will cost. Price negotiations should wait for a subsequent meeting. If they like your idea, they'll invite you back. At that time you can gather the information you need to price the venture accurately.

Sales is the creation of a mutually satisfying relationship. Each party wants something the other party has, and the sales meeting is the dance in which you arrange the exchange. Most of its steps are predictable: You know what they'll ask and you can rehearse the answers. Every once in a while something unpredictable happens. They offer the one response for which you weren't prepared. We call it a "window of weirdness." It's bound to happen. You can't avoid it. Still, it helps to anticipate that it *might* happen. So don't be devastated by it.

RULE OF THUMB

GET THEM EXCITED ABOUT YOUR IDEA FIRST,
THEN TELL THEM WHAT IT WILL COST.

BABY'S GOT A BRAND NEW PAIR OF SHOES

It also helps to remind yourself that you are your venture's best salesperson. Think about it. Who talked the babysitter into letting you stay up late? Who talked your parents into giving you the car keys when they didn't want to? You did—because you believed in what you were selling, and it showed. The same is true for your venture. No one will believe in it more strongly or communicate it with more enthusiasm than you will. In fact, your enthusiasm, because it's infectious, is your greatest sales tool.

CHECKLIST: TERMINOLOGY

It's important in sales meetings to talk the corporate language. That should remind your corporate contacts that you think like they do—in business terms. Start substituting these for-profit terms for their nonprofit equivalents.

FOR-PROFIT TERM	NONPROFIT EQUIVALENT
invest	*support*
investment	*donation*

FOR-PROFIT TERM	NONPROFIT EQUIVALENT
investor	*donor, funder*
partner	*sponsor*
profit	*surplus (or excess funds)*
return on investment	*well, it was good publicity!*

Also, note these internationally different terms.

UNITED KINGDOM TERM	UNITED STATES AND CANADIAN EQUIVALENT
charities	*nonprofit organizations*
companies	*corporations*
sponsorship	*marketing dollars*

SAMPLE FILE

TREES, INCORPORATED

Trees, Incorporated is a hypothetical environmental group. They have developed a portable exhibit on their area's ecology that they would like to rent to a shopping mall. Their director, Janet Casey, has secured a meeting with the director of the mall's merchant association, a guy named John Tara. Here's their conversation.

CASEY: I've made some assumptions about you. If they're correct, let's talk. If not, we're wasting each other's time. Assumption #1: You need to increase the traffic in the mall. Assumption #2: You need to increase your merchants' sales volume and their profits. Assumption #3: You want to show the community you're involved with their concerns. Assumption #4: You need to show your merchants that when you spend their marketing money you get a demonstrable return. Am I right?

TARA: True. You say Trees, Inc. is a nonprofit organization?

CASEY: Yes, why?

TARA: You don't sound like a nonprofit type, I mean... well, never mind, go ahead and finish your pitch.

CASEY: Okay. I've got something for you that is affordable, competitively priced, and exclusively yours. [Casey pauses.] You look skeptical.

TARA: [smiling] Maybe a little.

CASEY: I have a portable exhibit on our state's ecology. It can be at your mall Thursday through Sunday. It's a turnkey operation: We'll set it up, take it down, and staff it. Your staff will have no responsibilities. We'll advertise its visit to your mall in our newsletter, which is read by over five thousand people. According to surveys by *City Magazine,* this area has fifty thousand people who consider themselves "environmentalists." Seventy-two percent of them earn over $50,000 a year. We have a lot of credibility with these people, and many of them will visit the exhibit if you advertise it. Not only will they shop in your stores, they'll consider your center a friend of the cause. The exhibit will cost you $1,500 for the four days. I think you and your merchants will find that investment produces a measurable return. What do you say?

Casey has shown Tara that she knows the mall director's business. She's substantiated that he can attract desirable new customers. She's shown he can influence his community image, and how he can make himself look good to his merchants. All for only $1,500, which they both know is consistent with the mall's promotions budget.

How does Janet Casey know that? She knows because she's done her homework. She called three other malls and asked how they run promotions and how much they pay. She talked to three merchants about what they like in a promotion, and she talked to the Petting Zoo people who were at this mall last weekend to confirm what she'd learned.

From her own records she has already gleaned statistics on the environmentalist population in the area. That's Trees' target market and the main asset they can sell to a corporate partner. What about their newsletter? Trees has only 2,200 members, but its membership survey indicated that each issue of the newsletter is read by an average of 2.3 people. All this homework put Casey in a strong negotiating position in that sales meeting.

CHAPTER 28
THE PROPOSAL

SAN JOSE, CA: It took firefighters 20 minutes, using wire cutters and needle-nosed pliers, to free a woman from a pair of tight-fitting designer jeans. The woman had borrowed the pants from a cousin.
—THE *NEW YORK TIMES*

Know what you're getting into—and make it equally clear to your potential partner—by putting your proposal in writing. Your first corporate contact probably won't be your last; he will probably have to show it to his boss. Since you can't be at that meeting, you want a "stand-in" there, something that will present your venture in its most favorable light. That is your proposal.

THE FOUR-PAGE FITTING

The proposal is a short (four-page!) reminder of what you told your company contact in person. The first two pages are a narrative. They describe the venture in concrete terms and cover the five basic questions of sales (Chapter 27). The last two pages are pictures. They show the venture in action. If the venture is an event, they show people at it. If it's a product or service, they show people using it. People buy things they can visualize, so the proposal makes them visualize success.

The pictures can be simple, black-and-white line drawings, or quick magic marker sketches. They don't need to be fancy, but they must be professional quality and easy to read. They should display the company's name prominently on the product or service.

To get the pictures made inexpensively or for free, try the following sources:

- AN ARCHITECTURE FIRM. Architects are used to doing renderings and can do them quickly. In slow times, they may take on small pro bono (free) projects to keep their drafters busy.

- A CORPORATION with in-house design services. Ask for an in-kind donation.

- **VOCATIONAL SCHOOLS, COMMUNITY COLLEGES, OR ART SCHOOLS.** Renderings of ventures make great student projects.

- **AD AGENCIES, DESIGN FIRMS, AND PRINTERS.** They may do it for a nominal fee as a portfolio piece.

The point of the proposal is not to do a heavy pitch for your venture, but rather to remind your contact about its salient points and to act as a teaser for his or her boss. The proposal contains no long philosophies. No rationales. No budget. It succinctly paints a picture of your potential partnership's success. It makes the corporation an offer that looks to be a natural, comfortable, and valuable fit.

It is a tool to convince the corporation that they want to do business with you, and to get you back in the door to discuss the details of the deal. It should lead to a second meeting at which you discuss how to make the venture best meet both partners' needs, and how much it will cost to do so.

CHAPTER 29
RETAIL SALES

Once the toothpaste is out of the tube, it's hard to get it back in.
—H. R. HALDEMAN, AIDE TO PRESIDENT RICHARD NIXON

Try everything else first.

Until now this book has talked about wholesaling our products and services through corporations. That way there's a guaranteed sale, minimum cash outlay, no unsold inventory, low risk to you. It's the easiest, safest way to go.

Selling to the general public is risky. It requires a lot of money for manufacturing, warehousing, advertising, and selling the inventory—and you have no guarantee the merchandise will sell. You're no longer talking about doing a venture. You're talking about running a business.

You will require the same planning and capital as any start-up business; you'll also face the same risk. U.S. Commerce Department statistics show more than ninety percent of all new businesses fail within ten years, so we recommend you consider this route only after you have exhausted all preselling methods. If you do decide to retail, here are some things to consider.

WRITE A BUSINESS PLAN. Get experts in the field you are entering to help you develop a solid business plan before beginning. The plan will provide an operating path to follow in implementing the business, and will be a tool for raising cash from business partners or financial institutions. The plan should include four main points:

1. A STRATEGIC PLAN that explains the product or service's role in the marketplace and in the organization, and what its main business objectives will be.
2. AN OPERATIONAL PLAN that explains how the organization plans to implement the business.
3. A FINANCIAL PLAN that indicates projected expenses and income.
4. A CONTINGENCY PLAN that describes how the organization will handle unexpected events.

Several Internet sites will help you write a concise business plan, including www.dotcombizplan.com and the small business area of www.about.com. Your public library or local business school library will have many books on how to develop a business plan. Consult one of them for more specific information. A business school class might even be willing to develop a plan for you as a class project.

PROVIDE ADEQUATE CAPITAL. The major reason new businesses fail is because they are undercapitalized. Be sure you aren't. When you do your business plan *pro forma,* be conservative. Don't get caught six months into the business without adequate capital to meet the demand.

INSTALL A SOLID MANAGEMENT TEAM. The second reason new businesses fail is weak management. Do you have qualified, *experienced* managers to undertake this project? If not, find them. Without them, don't do the business.

CREATE "SAFETY NET" SALES. Even if you're confident about public sales, maximize your product or service's income potential by also selling it as a corporate premium item and/or selling it through a publisher or distributor. Plan to use it in-house as a membership inducement or fundraising premium. The more sales avenues you can create, the less risky the business will be.

NEGOTIATE A LICENSING AGREEMENT WITH A MANUFACTURER. This is the best way to reduce risk, although in exchange you sacrifice revenue. In a licensing agreement, you contract with a manufacturer to produce the product for you, with your name, logo, and information on it. The manufacturer also markets it and gives you a percentage of the sales. A number of nonprofits have successfully pursued this route:

- CHILDREN'S TELEVISION WORKSHOP licenses *Sesame Street* characters to manufacturers of children's clothing and products and nets several million dollars each year.

- THE CALIFORNIA GRAPE BOARD earned millions of dollars by licensing their advertising mascots, the California Raisins to manufacturers of everything from plush toys to radios.

Of course, the trick to licensing is having a product with large enough sales potential to be of interest to a manufacturer. A licensing agent can help connect you with a manufacturer, and help you negotiate the best deal.

Wave Hill is a nonprofit public garden and cultural institution located in the Bronx, New York. Wave Hill wanted to augment their funding and increase public awareness of the institution and its need for money. Administrators at Wave Hill decided to start a commercial venture selling lawn chairs like those used in their gardens.

The Wave Hill chair is based on the chair designed by architect Gerrit Rietveld, on display at the Museum of Modern Art. The Wave Hill gardening staff built the chairs specifically for display in the garden and to be given to donors of large gifts as a premium. Visitors to Wave Hill have admired them since they were first placed in the gardens twenty years ago.

Selling the chairs to the public seemed an excellent way to raise money and promote the organization. The staff had experience manufacturing the chairs and downtime during the winter in which to build them. Also, the popularity of the chairs indicated a viable market.

The business was operated by a small group of Wave Hill employees and was overseen by the director of development, who assumed responsibility after the first year of operation. The gardeners on the staff occasionally needed assistance from outside the operation since peak demand for the chair coincided with peak demand for the gardeners' time, spring and summer. The chairs were promoted in fliers and press releases that were sent to members, prospective customers, and newspapers. The business also received free national coverage in well-known publications such as the *New York Times* and *House Beautiful*. As a result, inquiries came in from people throughout the country.

But there was a major flaw in the business plan—there was no way to distribute the chairs. Shippers, like United Parcel Service, refused to deliver them fully assembled because they were too large. And disassembling the chair, in the opinion of the venture managers, compromised the quality of the product.

The venture managers considered selling the chairs through retail outlets, but decided against it because they felt they lost too much control over the product. Retailers wanted to charge prices for the chair the Wave Hill managers considered excessive. They feared this would have a negative impact on the organization's image.

According to Peter Sauer, the director of Wave Hill, "It was extremely difficult for us to tie into distribution channels because our operation is so small. We have little bargaining power with large companies." Ultimately, the chairs were distributed only in the metropolitan New York City area. They were delivered by members of the gardening staff for a fee, or picked up by customers directly from Wave Hill. Potential customers from outside the New York City area could get the chairs only if they made arrangements to have them delivered. Many sales were lost as a result. Despite their limited distribution, seventy-six chairs were sold in the first two years of operating and brought in revenue of $9,500. (Profit figures were not available.)

The chair was priced at $125, based on the approximate manufacturing costs. According to one source the price did not cover overhead and supervision, and probably did not cover the full labor cost, as it diverted employees from their work in the gardens.

Wave Hill's adventures in marketing its product have taken many turns over the years. Because of the problems they encountered and the unanticipated complexities of the operation, Wave Hill managers decided to search for alternative ways to keep the business alive without being directly involved. An arrangement was negotiated with a large seed and garden supply company, giving them the license to manufacture and market the chair for royalty fees. The garden supply company, which began selling the chair a year later, has the manufacturing, marketing, and distribution capabilities to successfully run the operation on a large scale.

Despite the problems, Mr. Sauer called the venture "an unqualified success. It achieved the objectives set at the start of the venture, that is, to generate income for the organization, and increased public awareness of Wave Hill."

As the venture managers at Wave Hill learned, it is vital to consider all aspects of marketing before commencing a venture. A great product and proven demand were not enough to assure the venture's success—*they also needed a way to get the product to the customer.* A marketing plan, its sophistication determined by the complexity of the venture, is essential to determine whether or not the organization has the resources, expertise, systems, and philosophy to make the venture a success.[5]

CHAPTER 30
NEW MARKETS FOR YOUR EXISTING PROGRAMS

As pretty as you are,
you know you could have been a flower;
If good looks was a minute,
you know you could have been an hour;
The way you stole my heart,
you know you could have been a cool crook;
And baby you're so smart,
you know you could have been a schoolbook.
—WM. ROBINSON AND B. ROGERS, "THE WAY YOU DO THE THINGS YOU DO"[6]

The Primes had an interesting sound. They just needed repackaging. They donned coordinated white, sequined outfits and added some smooth choreography to their act. Repackaged, they sold 22 million records worldwide and became one of the most successful rhythm and blues groups of all time: The Temptations. "The Way You Do The Things You Do," the anthem of repackaging, was their first hit.

Before you start thinking about developing new products, services, or special events, take a good look at what you already have. Chances are your assets include several hits just waiting to be heard. Don't sit on them. Whether they are physical or programmatic, repackage your assets for sale.

GETTING A HIGHER PRICE

Look at the programs you're now offering to a low-paying or nonpaying audience. Ask yourself who else might need or want them. Perhaps "Robin Hood Marketing" is in order. Can you sell those same programs at higher prices to more affluent markets? Vancouver Family Services was already doing counseling for low-income people. To increase their revenue and reach new populations they contracted with corporations to provide the same services to employees.

Impact House, a substance abuse agency in Pasadena, California, provides counseling and treatment for people with drug and alcohol problems. It is funded primarily by government contracts that don't pay the full cost of treatment. However, Impact House has begun offering the same services to corporations. Lockheed, Xerox, Pacific Bell, and other major employers pay Impact House up to $350 per day to counsel employees with drug and alcohol problems. The income has insured Impact House's financial stability.

REPACKAGING

Above, the nonprofit took a service it was already performing and sold it, unchanged, to a new, more affluent market. However, sometimes a sale to a new market requires repackaging and "repositioning" the product or service in order to better meet the new market's need.

The Bronx Frontier Development Corporation is a neighborhood self-help agency. Through neighborhood improvement projects it creates jobs. One of its projects was a community farm that grew and sold spices to hotels, cruise shops, and restaurants. The highest fixed expense of the farm was fertilizer, so in an attempt to cut costs, Frontier collected free manure from the Bronx Zoo. (For the zoo this was a great waste management solution.) The manure made excellent fertilizer, and before long, other neighborhood gardeners were asking if they could have some too. So the enterprising Frontier packaged "Zoo Doo" as a deluxe fertilizer for houseplants and gardens. The clever packaging caught the eye of Bloomingdale's, where it sold thirty thousand bags annually in catalog sales. Frontier has licensed the name to zoos around the country and makes royalties off their sales.

The Center in the Park, a senior service center in Philadelphia, offers low-cost field trips to its clients. The trips are highly popular, and the center frequently has to turn people away. To decrease demand for the trips—and to make money on them without increasing the charge to clients—the center created a CIP (Center in the Park) Card and repositioned the trips as a benefit for cardholders. The card, which costs $5, grossed $5,000 in its first few weeks.

Like so many nonprofit organizations in the late 1980s, the Wyman Center struggled to redefine what it does in order to expand its base of customers. Originally, Wyman was just a summer camp for underprivileged kids near St. Louis, Missouri. Utilizing consultants who specialize in helping corporations identify new markets, Wyman's CEO Dave Hilliard and his staff were able to clarify that what makes the camp special is not recreation, but the particular expertise the staff has in teaching children how to work in teams, to be leaders, and to resolve conflicts.

Over the next decade, Hilliard parlayed this new awareness into new camping options and then into a coherent and cohesive set of products and services that Wyman makes available to corporations, business forums, and schools. Today, Wyman programs have been franchised around the country and the organization is financially healthy and growing. The secret? Hilliard and his staff were able to repackage what Wyman offers into products and services that are attractive to constituencies willing to pay top dollar.

The Dallas Classical Guitar Society wanted to sell tapes of classical guitar music. To broaden their appeal, they positioned them as "romantic music for spending time with that special person." They packaged the tapes with a bottle of wine, two glasses, and a rose, and named the new product "Romance in a Box." They use the boxes as high-end membership premiums and wholesale them to liquor stores.

TAPPING PHYSICAL ASSETS

When your machines are turned off, what else could they be doing? When a space is empty, how could it be filled? Take a hard look at your physical assets to see if any can be used to generate revenue.

It's hard to believe that a hospital cafeteria could be known for good food, but that's the case at the Great Falls Hospital in Montana. The cafeteria also has downtimes between meal services when they could prepare extra food. So hospital administrators decided to capitalize on their asset. They opened a catering service, first catering just staff parties and now expanding to community functions.

Like most other nonprofits, the Sacramento Arts Commission has a phone machine that gives information about its programs and services. Unlike most others, it rents time on its line to local arts groups who use it to advertise their upcoming performances. In one stroke, the arts commission is performing its arts advocacy function and generating income!

WQED, the Pittsburgh public radio station, has a large library of classical and jazz CDs that it taps as a revenue source. For a fee, WQED will provide customized music for weddings, parties, or other events. They've even been contracted by the transit authority to package music for the new city subway system.

SEEING YOUR AUDIENCE FROM ALL SIDES

One of the most valuable but overlooked assets in a nonprofit is its audience. Most organizations contact thousands of people a year—users, donors, suppliers, and colleagues. Yet they miss their potential as income generators.

What most nonprofits fail to realize is that your current audience is your best audience. They're easy to reach, and they're ready to buy. It pays to give them plenty of chances.

You can do this by thinking of your audience as a rectangle. Before you jump to conclusions, hear us out. Most people will come to your organization in one of four ways:

1. As members
2. As donors
3. As buyers (of a product or service)
4. As visitors (to a special event)

Too often, nonprofits isolate these groups. Donors are invited to certain events, members to others, and the general public to yet others. The groups are treated as if they were eligible for only one type of relationship with the organization. They're not!

Your real job is to try to win each group over into the other three categories. If you think of each of these "entry" points as the corner of a rectangle, your job is to slide everybody around to the other three corners.

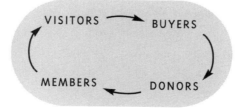

First make sure each of the "entry" experiences is positive so everyone will want to come back. Then give them regular and appealing opportunities to do so. Create a varied menu of opportunities to associate with you throughout the year, including chances to buy products or services, invitations to attend events, opportunities to join, and requests for donations.

Then make sure everyone in all four categories is invited to everything. To do this, you'll have to capture complete names and addresses of every contact. Log them on a computerized database that can sort by type of contact (donor, member, etc.) and merge lists. Then mail materials to all your contacts at least three times a year.

SAMPLE FILE

NATIONAL GEOGRAPHIC SOCIETY

The National Geographic Society is a master at this. Their magazine reaches millions of people who pay to read about the world around them. But why just read about it? National Geographic goes back to those subscribers with games, calendars, videotapes, a children's magazine, and other items—all spin-offs of their basic product.

SAMPLE FILE

MINNESOTA PUBLIC RADIO

Minnesota Public Radio has done the same thing a different way. They are the folks who brought you *A Prairie Home Companion,* and they knew a loyal audience when they heard one. They tapped their audience with an annual catalog of *Prairie Home Companion*—related merchandise.

The catalog operation has expanded considerably from its early days when boxes of T-shirts bulged from under desks. It's become a for-profit subsidiary, the Riverton Trading Company. Their database is attractive to advertisers, so MPR launched a magazine that generates ad revenue. MPR recently sold the Riverton Trading Company enterprise to Dayton-Hudson for $120 million and put $90 million into an endowment for the public radio network.

They've recently tapped their audience one more

ACCESSING YOUR NETWORK

Equally as important as your users may be your peer organizations. What networks are you in? To whom do you have access? By networking with other organizations you may be able to create a purchasing group with a lot of clout.

SAMPLE FILE

SWIM B.C.

Swim B.C. is the Canadian nonprofit that promotes recreational and competitive swimming. Its single center in Vancouver serves several hundred thousand people annually—a respectable number, but peanuts compared to the seven million Canadians who swim recreationally each year. How to reach those seven million? How to capitalize on their interest in swimming? Swim B.C. is organizing other centers across Canada to create a national network of swim centers.

Through the network, they'll have access to millions of Canadian swimmers to whom they'll market a private line of merchandise called "Otterwear." The products will be sold in "aquatic boutiques" in each center, through a mail-order catalog, and retail. A portion of each sale will go to Swim B.C. and a portion will stay with the center that made the sale.

OPTIMIZING YOUR BUILDING AND GROUNDS

Another valuable asset may be your building and/or grounds. Whose needs can they meet besides your own? Are there long hours when you're not in your building? Are there groups in town that need rehearsal space? Meeting space? Party space? Classroom space?

Space and ground rental can be an easy, low-cost way to generate income. Just make sure you've covered all your costs in making the space available—heat, lights, staff, security, insurance, etc., plus a profit—before you sign a lease.

Given the nature of its collection, it's not surprising that the Museum of Outdoor Art in Greenwood Village, Colorado, has a lot of land. What is surprising is the way they've used it to generate income. A section of the property forms a natural amphitheater and the museum had, from time to time, rented the area to the Denver Symphony and other groups for staging concerts. But the rentals were sporadic and the income inconsistent.

When a friend of the museum's attended an entertainment promoters conference and heard that the developing trend among concert promoters was to rent alternative, non-auditorium-style arenas, the museum realized they were literally sitting on a gold mine. They contacted MCA, the entertainment conglomerate that organizes national concert tours, and proposed their site as the Denver setting for a season's concerts.

MCA liked the idea. They gave the museum money to codevelop the site with seating and a professional stage, and the two organizations signed a lucrative contract for several seasons of big name rock, folk, and jazz concerts. The museum has expanded the venture by joining with a nearby Hyatt Hotel to offer a concert/hotel package. Buyers receive discount hotel accommodations with their concert ticket, and the museum gets a percentage of each sale.

Historic Denver, the city's historic preservation organization, owns and operates the Molly Brown House, home of the unsinkable Victorian hostess. One strategy that keeps Historic Denver afloat is space rental in Molly's house.

The organization rents out the third floor ballroom for Victorian dinners, lunches, and high teas. The food, authentic dishes from turn-of-the-century Denver, is served by volunteers wearing reproduction costumes from the period, amidst authentic table decorations and period furnishings. The fee includes a tour of the house and a brief background on Victorian society.

Amazingly, the entire operation is run by volunteers under the supervision of the Molly Brown House director. The fifteen volunteers who organize, cook, and serve the meals are all on three-year contracts with the organization. At the rate of one meal every other week, they are barely able to keep up with demand, so Historic Denver has considered contracting the service to a caterer in order to accommodate more parties.

For the organization, the meals offer steady income, especially during the winter when the House serves fewer tourists. They also provide a popular and engaging way to teach Denver history. The organization also rents the ballroom without the meals, but fewer people select that option. Renters prefer the elegant parties and authentic Victorian atmosphere they provide. After all, that's what visiting the Molly Brown House is all about.

"BUNDLING" PROGRAMS

Robert Carr and Johnny Mitchell, two Bronx, New York, teenagers, had been singing solo without much success. But when they harmonized together, they sounded great. Together, they spent twenty-two weeks on the national music charts with the 1958 "bundling" classic, *We Belong Together*.

There are times when you can increase the salability of your products and services by "bundling" two or more together. Each benefits from the added value of the other. Appropriately, we call this the "Robert & Johnny Effect."

SAMPLE FILE

COLORADO PUBLIC RADIO

Colorado Public Radio and its Denver station, KCFR, used bundling to package a summer concert series. They knew their listeners would enjoy live jazz and classical concerts, but they had no facility in which to hold them. They could have rented a local concert hall, but that didn't add sizzle to the event. Instead, they "bundled" their concerts with the attractive outdoor amphitheater of the Denver Botanic Gardens, and the result was one of the most popular summer events in the city. Tickets to the annual series of outdoor concerts usually sold out within hours of going on sale.

SAMPLE FILE

ROCKY MOUNTAIN INSTITUTE

The Rocky Mountain Institute used "bundling" to create a whole new way to sell their services. RMI does research and consulting on economic renewal. They offer a variety of services designed to revitalize communities by strengthening local business. Sold separately, the services were slow movers.

So RMI bundled their services into a package called "Competitek." A Competitek package had a fixed price, lasted exactly one year, and offered an attractive blend of services. The combined services offered a comprehensive solution to a community's economic problems, making the package more desirable. As a result, packaged services came to generate a substantial portion of RMI's income. An added benefit to RMI was efficiency. Whereas before RMI staff spent a lot of time pushing many small sales, they now had to make fewer sales that had a much bigger payoff.

An update: In the 1990s, RMI transformed this effort into a for-profit company called E-Source. After six years of operation, E-Source was sold for $18 million, producing nearly $1 million annually in evergreen funding for RMI.

CHAPTER 31
MAKING THE PROMISE REAL

The whole idea is to deliver what money can't buy.
—BRUCE SPRINGSTEEN, IDOL

TALL TIMBERS TO TOOTHPICKS, THE DUMMY DOESN'T LAST LONG

Edgar Bergen and Charley McCarthy were stars on radio, but with the advent of television they faded. Was it because Edgar was the kind of ventriloquist who needed radio to gloss over his moving lips? The point is, once you're out in the open with a promise, you've got to perform.

In creating a vision for your organization, you've made a promise—to yourselves, to your investors, and to your publics. You've told them where you're going in the next few years, what you plan to achieve, and some of the paths you will take to get there. Now you have to make that promise real. You have to give people concrete evidence that you're doing what you said you would.

Each of your products, services, and special events is a realization of the promise. Each one should demonstrate to the public that you are moving toward your goals. The Denver Children's Museum "promised" to provide high-quality educational products and services for families, and followed through with publications, traveling exhibits, and special events that encouraged families to play and learn together. The National Crime Prevention Council "promised" to help America take a bite out of crime, and followed through with print materials, media campaigns, and community and corporate action kits that give citizens the tools for fighting crime in their work sites, homes, and neighborhoods.

Each of your products, services, and special events should do the same for you. Each one should be directly related to the vision you created. Each should be one more demonstration that you are making that promise real.

STANDIN' BY YOUR CANON

Your promise doesn't stop there. You've also promised your public that you would be customer centered and that you would be the best organization in your area of specialty. Now you have to look for ways to realize those goals. Swope Health Center wanted to realize its promise to be "the best health clinic for modest-income people," so they repainted the stripes in their parking lot. They painted "staff only" green stripes far away from the door, reserving the close-in spaces for patients. It was a literal way of saying to patients, "You come first."

RULE OF THUMB

IF YOU CAN'T MAKE IT TOP QUALITY, DON'T DO IT.

Look at all the places in your organization where customer contact happens—at your front counter, in your billing operation, and in the delivery of your primary services. Are all those contacts making your promise real?

You've segmented your audience in order to meet individual group's needs. Now look at your organization from each group's point of view. Do you say you want Spanish-speaking customers, but post signs only in English? Do you say you want families at your programs, but offer most of your programs on weekdays? Look at all the messages your organization puts out—implicit as well as explicit. What promises are you making, and what are you really delivering?

The same kind of scrutiny should be applied to every communication that travels out your front door. Everything you send into the world is a complete picture of your organization to the person who sees it—from business letters to your van on the highway. For some people, that one communication may be the only "message" they ever see! So make it count. Make sure every contact is an accurate, engineered reflection of your organization. Make each convey the promise you've made to the public—to be the best organization in your field.

Print materials and Web sites are as important as activities. If you can't make it top quality, don't do it. Too often, nonprofits confuse slick with professional. They fear that expensive-looking print pieces will make them look too well endowed to attract funds. Freeze that assumption! Poverty doesn't sell; professionalism does. Each piece must remind the public that you're making your quality promise real.

KEEPING YOUR CONTACT VISCERAL

Part of making the promise real is communicating. It's not enough to offer quality products and services. You have to tell consumers you're doing it. It's not enough to improve the quality of customer contact. You have to tell potential customers about it. As you strengthen your ability to make good on your promises, take every opportunity to spread that message.

To do that effectively and inexpensively, ask each of your corporate partners to advertise your ventures in their own ads, mailers, newsletters, and on their Web sites. It strengthens their association with you and lets you reach broad audiences for free. Ask corporations that have shied away from joint ventures with you to include information about you and your entrepreneurial efforts in their communications. By, for example, featuring you on their Web site as a community service, they will gain some of the benefit of a joint venture without the expense. Ask grocery stores to print messages from you on their paper bags. They will benefit from the association; you will reach thousands of people with discount coupons (for products, services, or special events), with half-price membership offers, or with some other organizational message.

In a sense, once you become an entrepreneurial, customer-centered organization, every contact with the public becomes an inducement, a reason to get closer to you—a chance for a sale, now or in the future. Each contact should remind them how you can meet their needs.

RULE OF THUMB

ONCE YOU BECOME AN ENTREPRENEURIAL ORGANIZATION, EVERY CONTACT WITH THE PUBLIC BECOMES A CHANCE FOR A SALE.

CHAPTER 32
A TIMELINE

We know that as a people, we must seize our time.
—BOBBY SEALE, BLACK PANTHER, CHICAGO 8 MEMBER,
BARBECUE COOKBOOK AUTHOR

My protest days are over.
—JERRY RUBIN, YIPPIE, CHICAGO 8 MEMBER, NIGHTCLUB PARTY PRODUCER

I was political then, I'm political now.
—LEE WEINER, SOCIOLOGY TEACHER, CHICAGO 8 MEMBER,
NONPROFIT ENTREPRENEUR

How long should this whole process take? From the time you become serious about enterprise and administer the questionnaire to the time you start pitching your first venture to a corporation should take about ninety days. Once you start, it's important to keep the momentum going.

By the end of thirty days you should have completed your vision and should have strong visuals and a slogan ready to show potential corporate partners.

By the end of sixty days you should have narrowed your list of possible ventures to the top three first choices, and you should be checking those three against the nine criteria (see chapter 20).

By the end of ninety days you should have selected your first venture, you should have its proposal ready, and you should be making appointments with corporate decision makers to pitch it.

It's not long from there until your first venture is operational and you're planning number two. By now you should be viewing everything with an entrepreneurial eye.

That's an ambitious schedule, but enterprise is a fast-paced game. If you can't move quickly now, you'll have a hard time keeping up later. Within three to five years, your old, pre-entrepreneurial organization should be just a memory to you, your audience, and your community.

PART V

VEHICLES: DRIVING THE FANTASY HOME

CHAPTER 33
INTRODUCING ENTERPRISE INTO YOUR ORGANIZATION

You've created a vision of entrepreneurial organization. You've developed ideas for ventures the organization can do. This part of the book will give you the vehicles for implementing both. You've done the hard, creative work. This is the mechanics, the systems and structures that will help you integrate enterprise smoothly into your organization.

WELCOME TO THE NEW WORLD

In 1928, according to Gary Cooper, he and actress Nancy Carroll were shooting the last scenes of *The Shopworn Angel* for Paramount Pictures when, for the first time, sound was available to filmmakers. Paramount wanted to be part of the new technology immediately. So a bit of dialogue was added. "I studied my script containing this new thing called dialogue," Cooper told the *Saturday Evening Post,* "until it was letter perfect." In the film's closing seconds, a wedding scene, the first and only words were uttered:

COOPER: "I do."

CARROLL: "I do."

With those four words the picture was released as a talkie, seizing the opportunity to grow with the times.

LOW COMMOTION

If your organization is like most nonprofits, it won't be used to entrepreneurial behaviors. You'll be asking people who are used to reacting to customers' demands to proactively seek out those customers' needs. You may be asking a system that is used to consensus decision making to streamline its own inefficient-but-comfortable process. Most difficult of all, you will be asking an organization that thinks solely about service to start thinking about making money.

None of these behaviors will come quickly or easily. You are asking people to accept some fundamental changes in the way their organization runs, and change is frightening. They will need to be educated about the new direction and why it's happening, and treated patiently as they learn the new behaviors.

It helps to recognize that this is not the first time your organization has changed. Organizations go through many stages as they grow—from infancy to adolescence to maturity. At each stage people leave because the organization is no longer the one they chose to work in. The introduction of enterprise is one more stage. For some staff it will be a natural progression. They will adapt readily, they will relish the change. Others may never accept it. Let them go. They will be happier in a more traditional nonprofit.

THE FEAR THAT BLINDS

The greatest fear in organizations that turn to enterprise is that quality will be sacrificed for money. Staffs fear that the organization will lose its mission in its desire to earn money, that money will become an end in itself, rather than merely a means to get there. Recognize this fear and address it. It is fear that often is seen and manifested in political infighting. Beware! Encourage people to express their concern so it doesn't fester underground. Then patiently explain your own concern for quality.

Plan to spend a lot of time educating your staff about enterprise. Just as you need to actively communicate your changes to the outside world, you need to do "internal marketing" with your staff and board. Remind them how enterprise furthers the organization's mission, how it enables you to reach new audiences, how it earns money to subsidize programs that won't pay for themselves.

Assure them that money will be a means to an end, never an end in itself. Assure them that you won't sacrifice quality for money, that the quality of programs will be nonnegotiable. The people who create programs now should be among the designers and implementers of your new programs; they should see those programs as furthering what they do now. They must work closely with enterprise staff to set goals and standards. They must be your voices of quality control.

PREDICTABLE PROBLEMS

There will be some tension between your programs and enterprise staffs. That is unavoidable. Programs staff will push for programs the enterprise staff can't sell. That's okay: Pursue your traditional sources of funding for those. Enterprise staff will push for some projects your programs staff dislikes. That is also okay, let them battle it out. The debates between them are healthy! They will force you to constantly reexamine your goals and your means of achieving them. Because of this tension, entrepreneurial organizations are dynamic places. They never become rusty or out of touch with their audiences. Their mission and visions don't get locked in bottom drawers. They never become complacent.

Tensions only become a problem when they are underground, so be sensitive to them. Watch for people who consistently make trouble. Some longtime staffers may be unwilling to adjust to the changes, yet unwilling to leave the organization. They may rebel against the organization by instigating political infighting. Be aware of it. Don't let it continue. Staff people who cannot make peace with the new ways can poison the organization. You may be faced with the difficult decision of terminating someone who has been a valuable member of the staff, but if your organization is serious about its new direction, don't hesitate. Both the organization and the individual will be better off.

TEAM RESOLVE

If you take your job of educating staff seriously, you should find the acceptance level high. Enterprise is an exciting process! It can bring you closer to your goals than you ever hoped. Most organizations that choose this route find it a unifying factor for their staffs; people are galvanized by the vision and become eager to implement it. They find that as they decide which corporations to work with and which to avoid, which ventures to pursue and which to refuse, not everyone agrees with every decision. But everyone believes in the organization's commitment to enterprise and, thus, its commitment to its mission.

SAMPLE FILE

ONTARIO SCIENCE CENTER

The Ontario Science Center in Toronto has long been a leader in the development of interactive science exhibits. As such, they receive frequent requests to develop exhibits for other centers. Recognizing the potential, and faced with the prospect of declining government subsidies, the center decided to pursue exhibit development and fabrication as an income-generating activity.

For their initial venture, they chose to market a set

of topology puzzles that are extremely popular at the center. Each puzzle has two to four clear acrylic pieces held together with rope. As the puzzler tries to separate the plastic pieces by twisting and sliding them around each other, he explores the relationship of surfaces that forms the basis of topology. Science Center staff had manufactured the puzzle pieces that were used at the center. But when they investigated commercial fabrication of the pieces, a puzzle of a different kind surfaced.

The Science Center puzzles contained several cylindrical parts. To have those pieces manufactured commercially would be quite expensive. Cheaper, and equally serviceable, would be to manufacture each cylindrical piece as a flat shape. The center commissioned a trial set of puzzles with the new flattened shapes, and when they came back from the manufacturer, the staff was unhappy. The puzzles still accomplished their purpose, although they had lost the satisfying feeling of holding a cool, smooth, acrylic cylinder in the palm of your hand. The puzzles still worked, but they had lost their aesthetic.

What to do? On the one hand, to realize the largest possible profit margin, the center wanted the lowest possible fabrication cost. On the other hand, they were committed to the quality of their product. After much debate, they chose the more expensive cylinders. They felt the puzzle had to represent the Science Center to the world and, therefore, had to be up to their usual standard. In fact, they decided, the increased quality would enhance sales. They willingly shrank their profit margin for the sake of quality.

SAMPLE FILE

AMERICAN GLOBAL RELEAF

The environmental organization American Forests has experienced many of the challenges of growing into an entrepreneurial organization. But they have also enjoyed the excitement of new ventures and new partnerships. The Global ReLeaf campaign was initiated to mobilize a massive tree-planting effort. It targeted landscapes damaged by hurricanes, floods, wildfires, and human abuses. American Forests knew they had an opportunity to approach corporate partners with an environmental action initiative that was positive, tangible, and nonconfrontational.

The staff developed one creative proposal after another. At fruition, American Forests developed a four-pronged approach to corporate partnerships: They wanted partners to promise general support for the organization, not just the Global ReLeaf effort. They wanted corporations to ally themselves with specific tree-planting initiatives, making sure they would have a noticeable impact on the nation's forests (more than five million trees have been planted in more than sixty Global ReLeaf sites). American Forests also expected corporate partners to invest in their education programs, distributing information to customers, employees, and the public. And, finally, the staff saw a role for indirect support, asking corporate partners in Global ReLeaf to provide advertising space on Web sites and in publications, and to purchase ad space in *American Forests* magazine as well.

American Forests articulated a clear and cohesive proposal for corporate partners. They provided tangible incentives for participation, and they followed through. Enterprise in the form of the Global ReLeaf corporate partnership effort had enlivened the organization with a vision of venture success.

CHAPTER 34
CREATING A DEPARTMENT
OF ENTERPRISE

Bureaucracy defends the status quo long past the time when
the quo has lost its status.
—LAURENCE PETER, OF THE PETER PRINCIPLE

CLOGGED FUEL LINES

Every day in the United States the federal government issues another one hundred pages of rules and regulations, while in the same day, six million tons of manure hit the ground behind farm animals.[7] Make of that what you will and trust your animal instincts; don't let yourself get clogged or bloated with bureaucracy. No matter how excited you are about enterprise, your organization harbors a lifetime of non-entrepreneurial habits. To succeed, your ventures must be sheltered from them. Ventures must be given protection by the executive director and freedom to be different from other organizational projects.

Ventures need distance from some of the operating rules of the organization, yet they need intimacy with others. The ventures will be furthering your mission. They will convey your spirit, philosophy, and quality. They will rely on your staff for quality checks, program support, and advice. Achieving this balance between distance and closeness is one of the primary challenges of introducing enterprise to your organization.

INDEPENDENT SUSPENSION

Start by installing a department of enterprise or a department of marketing on a par with your other major departments or divisions. Have it report to the executive director or chief administrator, and make its director part of the top management team. That way it has room to maneuver somewhat independently, yet is tied to your other departments and has a clear position in the organization's hierarchy.

Then allow the department to create its own rules. It will need to be more responsive to external demands than your organization is used to being, so it will need the freedom and resources to respond quickly and successfully.

Keep the following in mind as you install your department of enterprise:

DON'T TIE THE DEPARTMENT DOWN to the same layers of decision making that exist elsewhere in your organization. If unnecessary people get into the process, they bog it down. Enterprise demands streamlined decisions, not the "tyranny of democracy."

LET THE DEPARTMENT HIRE AND FIRE ITS OWN STAFF. The director of enterprise will have a better sense of the skills needed than someone used to hiring for a nonprofit. Give him or her the freedom to hire the skills he needs.

LET THE DEPARTMENT RECOMMEND ITS OWN SYSTEM OF SALARY INCEN-TIVES AND REWARDS. The salary issue is a tricky one. Enterprise staff may need to be hired from the private sector, where they are accustomed to higher salaries than you currently pay. This naturally causes some resentment in other staff. While there is no way to eliminate this conflict immediately, there are some things you can do to mitigate it:

- Use a system of incentives and rewards to compensate enterprise staff for accepting lower salaries than they are used to making.

- Use the introduction of enterprise and its resulting earned income to raise all salaries to higher levels.

- Offer all staff the opportunity to increase earnings with a system of incentives and rewards (see Chapter 36).

LET THE DEPARTMENT CONTROL ITS OWN CASH FLOW. The department will need access to cash irregularly and immediately. Make that access possible.

SUBSIDIARY INSULATION

Creating a department that operates differently from others in the organization is not easy. It places a great deal of responsibility on the executive director to justify the differences and to minimize resentment between the enterprise department and others. For this reason, some organizations choose to incorporate their departments of enterprise as nonprofit subsidiaries. This makes it structurally easier to create different rules for the division. It also has several other advantages. It insulates your organization from liability should a venture turn sour. It protects your nonprofit status if the enterprise activity is deemed unrelated to your mission. And a separate for-profit-minded subsidiary may more easily attract corporate partners.

The subsidiary can be nonprofit or for-profit, depending on the types of ventures it plans to do. Small ventures directly related to your mission are best handled in a nonprofit corporation. Larger, ongoing, less closely related ventures should be handled by a for-profit. Consult a tax attorney who is familiar with nonprofit enterprise if you are considering pursuing this route.

The concern in creating a subsidiary is that it becomes too removed from the mission, spirit, and service-oriented nature of the organization. If subsidiary staff are not functionally part of the organization, if they don't interact daily with the organization's staff, will they be able to implement projects that reflect the organization's integrity and quality?

There is no right or wrong answer to this question. Each organization must choose the path that fits it best. Whichever route you choose, treat your new department with care. It takes a lot less to kill a new effort than to nourish it, and enterprise will seem more foreign and risky than most. Nurture it all you can.

CHAPTER 35
STAFFING THE DEPARTMENT OF ENTERPRISE

Said the Queen, "Now here, you see, it takes all the running you can do to keep in the same place. If you want to get somewhere else, you must run at least twice as fast as that!"
—CHARLES "LEWIS CARROLL" DODGSON, *THROUGH THE LOOKING GLASS*

"Staff a new department?!" you say. "Now you're really talking fantasy. We can't afford that." Relax.

Initially all you need in a department of enterprise is a director. He or she can work closely with the chief administrator and programs staff to conceive ventures and sell them. Once they're sold, he or she can hire contract staff to implement them. You don't need to hire additional staff until the work for the department has outgrown the director's time constraints.

A DIRECTOR: THE ART OF THE KEEL

Hiring the director, however, is critical. For enterprise to succeed, the department must have a full-time (or very close to full-time) champion, a captain who gives the department backbone and direction; someone whose primary responsibility is to sell ventures and see them through implementation. If you give the job to someone wearing another hat, the job won't get properly done. Enterprise demands a different outlook, a different set of skills than anyone in our organization may be currently using. To ask someone to do his or her existing, traditional job plus this new and different one is unfair and unrealistic.

The person you're looking for may already be on staff. If you've designated an enterprise champion, that person is most likely your candidate. If so, peel off his or her other responsibilities so he or she can concentrate on enterprise. In some organizations the executive director functions as the director of enterprise. This may work for a short time, while the process is just being launched, but once the work demands serious concentration and special skills, most executive directors find it necessary to hire someone else. Sometimes delaying your decision can take the organization dangerously off course, severely hampering the organization.

When you hire a director of enterprise, what qualities should you look for? You need someone with a foot in both camps, nonprofit and for-profit; someone who will love and honor your mission, and at the same time understand the bottom line and think like a businessperson. Not an easy person to find—but possible.

First and foremost, look for someone who understands and values your mission. Your director will need to promote the mission in every venture, so he or she has to believe in it wholeheartedly. Second, look for someone who is familiar with business and can apply business principles to a nonprofit. Third, look for someone who enjoys sales. Half the director's job will be creative: conceiving ventures, looking for partnership opportunities, working with staff to find ways the organization can tap market opportunities. The other half will be sales: cold calls and follow-up sales calls to get your ventures sold. This second half is important. You need to hire someone who genuinely likes selling, who isn't a programs person waiting for the right job to open.

QUALITIES TO LOOK FOR IN YOUR DIRECTOR OF ENTERPRISE

1. ORIENTED TOWARD SALES, NOT PUBLIC RELATIONS. PR people leave a meeting wanting everyone to feel good. Salespeople leave a meeting knowing quantities, prices, and delivery dates.

2. TOLERANCE FOR AMBIGUITY. Sales involves indecision, competing interests, and shifting priorities. The job is not for someone who needs one right answer and wants it right away.

3. WILLINGNESS TO RISK FAILURE AND REJECTION. You'll never make every sale. Just learn from every experience.

4. STRONG ORGANIZATIONAL SKILLS. Salespeople have their fingers in a lot of pots. They're constantly scouting the marketplace, prospecting leads, tracking past leads and clients, following up contacts, and working with suppliers to understand and deliver the product or service. It takes someone well organized and systematic.

5. INTEGRITY. Your salesperson should love your organization and its mission; should understand and believe in what he or she sells; and should

promise only what the organization can deliver.

6. ENTHUSIASM. Enthusiasm is infectious. It will be one of his or her strongest sales tools.

7. ENJOYS SOLVING PROBLEMS. The job of sales is really a problem-solving exercise. It involves listening to a corporation's problems and looking for ways your organization's expertise or creativity can meet them.

8. OPTIMISM. Good salespeople see opportunities where other see problems. They tend to be upbeat and positive.

9. RESOURCEFULNESS. Sales requires the ability to think quickly on your feet. Look for someone who's a creative thinker.

10. SENSE OF HUMOR. Laughter can lighten tense meetings and can see someone through when the "no's" seem overwhelming.

11. ABILITY TO LISTEN. If you're going to match your product or service with a corporation's need, you'd better listen well to the need. Good sales people know that the more they listen, the smarter they look.

12. GENUINELY LIKES PEOPLE. When it comes right down to it, sales is relationships between people. People buy from people, not from institutions. If you like people, it shows.

13. ARTICULATE. Look for someone who can explain your vision clearly and without jargon.

14. HIGH ENERGY LEVEL. You need someone action-oriented, eager to make the next call, and willing to try again after rejection; someone who can maintain a grueling level of activity without becoming unreasonably grumpy.

15. COMPETITIVE. Good salespeople are mildly impatient. They want results and try not to let it show...too much!

NAVIGATING RELATIONSHIPS

If your board is reluctant to create a new position, hire the director of enterprise on contract. If you're hiring someone new to the organization, this will give you both a chance to test the waters. It may also make it easier to hire the best person for the job, since the right candidate may have other commitments to fulfill before joining you full time and long term. Remember, through, no flirting with enterprise! Your commitment to the strategy must be long term even if the contract isn't.

Consider making the contract "no cut." That is, include a clause that says the director can't be fired if they're first (or even first few) ventures fail. They will need some room to take risks, and they won't have it if they're worried about losing their job to a failure. Consider including that clause in the executive director's contract as well. Especially if your board is nervous about enterprise, the added security will bolster your willingness to experiment and strengthen your ventures.

What is the relationship between the director of enterprise and the executive director? One of trust! You hire someone who understands your values and goals, who shares your vision and has the skills to implement it entrepreneurially. Then you let him or her go. That doesn't mean you turn your back and stop asking questions. It means you don't try to control the division's operations. As with leadership, you give direction but not directions. You provide a "spiritual check" for the enterprise director's activities, but you recognize that some of the means to the end may not be ones you would choose. After all, this business is probably new to you too.

THE CREW

While your department needs only a director initially, your ventures will require additional staff. Some may require skills you have in-house; others may require new ones. Some may need publications expertise; others, special events experience. Some may require professional qualifications; others may just need common sense. Don't lock yourself into needing a particular set of skills just because you have a person with those skills on staff. Don't pay high salaries for a year when you only need the skills for a month. And don't pay benefits when you don't need to at all.

Hire people on contract. Hire exactly the skills you need for as long as you need them. Go to the top of each field and hire the best people for the job. Don't forget that it was you who created a vision that says you are the best organization in your field. Now use the best people around to help you prove it.

Whatever you do, don't believe that you can't afford top-quality people. That's the old nonprofit way of thinking—that second-class mind-set. You can afford them. Experienced, high-priced professionals frequently do the job in half the time of their lower-priced colleagues. Also, you're looking at a short-term contract, not a long-priced salary. Write their professional costs into the venture's sales price. If you still feel you can't afford professionals, offer them equity shares in your venture; when the project sells, they collect a percentage of the sale. Remember, if you're the best in your field, you attract the best in others. Find creative ways to produce the excellence you promise.

FLAGS

More and more, nonprofits are giving conventional business titles to their staff positions. This is a good idea. It immediately communicates to your corporate contacts what your job levels and responsibilities are, and it's one more way to wave your message of "we mean business." Consider using these terms in place of traditional ones:

NONPROFIT TITLE	CORPORATE EQUIVALENT
Executive Director, Managing Director	President/Chief Executive Officer (CEO)
(Marketing) Director	Vice President of Marketing
President of the Board	Chair of the Board
Vice President of the Board	Vice Chair of the Board

CHAPTER 36
ENTERPRISE INSTIGATORS

That power, which erring men call Chance.
—JOHN MILTON, *PARADISE LOST*

RETURN OF THE HICKEY

Remember when you used to take chances? Luck had very little to do with it. There was the thrill of pushing your own expectations, then there was the genuine satisfaction as you accomplished beyond accepted limits. As with the mythic hickey of high school—wherein you proved your desirability without losing physical or emotional sanctity—you are now once again in a position to make your mark.

Unfortunately, nonprofits are traditional old biddies who subscribe (we would like to hope unwittingly) to a host of counterproductive operating assumptions. Most of these bromides sound so "normal." In fact, they have become bloody endemic; you never think to question them! Salaries are low, people burn out, money doesn't have to be generated in *our* department. That's the way life is in a nonprofit, dear.

Phooey! Good fortune must be sought. That's why entrepreneurial nonprofits are challenging these assumptions, and as a result, have found ways to replace the traditional behaviors with new, more productive ones. Here are some of the enterprise behaviors these progressive nonprofits are using. Adopting them will help you cultivate enterprise thinking in your staff and will speed your return to the ranks of risk takers.

ATTITUDES ABOUT MONEY

Typically, nonprofit staff don't think in terms of making and saving money. Each department is given a budget—and spends it. No attention is given to making money except in the department directly responsible for bringing it in, and attention to cost cutting occurs only at the end of the fiscal year in a last-ditch effort to end the year in the black.

Even at budget planning time, there are no incentives to make or save money. In most nonprofits, the new budget for each department starts from zero, as if it were its first year of operation. Money saved or earned the year before is forgotten. Collective amnesia sets in. Doesn't provide much incentive to make money or save it, does it?

Change this way of thinking by creating incentives for the department to make and save money.

CREATE A DEPARTMENT "ENTERPRISE FUND." If a department shows a surplus at the end of the year, let them keep fifty percent of it for their own discretionary use.

CREATE AN ORGANIZATION-WIDE PROFIT-SHARING PLAN. Provide an incentive for all staff to make and save money by creating an organization-wide profit-sharing plan. Take a predetermined percentage of the net profit at the end of the year and distribute it to staff based on time worked. Full-time employees get a full share, half-time employees a half share. The plan will also emphasize that all departments work toward overall organizational success and will partially offset low staff salaries.

BREAKING OLD HABITS

Too often, nonprofit people get in the habit of doing things the same old way. The problems never seem to change, neither do the solutions. This complacency makes it difficult to see changes in your markets or to institute new programs, and makes it almost impossible to take risks. Not only is this anti-entrepreneurial thinking, it fosters lassitude and burnout in your staff. Instead, you need to actively promote creative thinking and risk taking; make it safe to do so.

INSTITUTE "CREATIVITY AWARDS." Charles House, an engineer at Hewlett-Packard, won H-P's "Medal of Defiance" by pursuing an idea for an advanced picture tube—despite a kill order from management! Create your own version of the defiance award to actively encourage staff to try new things.

DESIGNATE A "PROBLEM OF THE MONTH." Each month publicize an organizational problem that's looking for a solution (perhaps an area in which you would like to cut costs or generate additional revenue). Ask employees to offer two bold, imaginative solutions—one that would cost money and one that would not. Offer a prize for the winning solution: dinner for two for a non-monetary solution, half the first year's savings or earnings for one that makes or saves money.

COMPETITIVE SALARIES AND REWARDS

One of the most valuable benefits of enterprise is that it provides unrestricted operating cash that can go toward raising salaries. Your goal should be to offer salaries competitive with the private sector. Announce that to the staff, and as enterprise makes it possible, institute across-the-board annual raises.

In the meantime, supplement salaries with a variety of institutional benefits.

OFFER INTEREST-FREE LOANS. Staff members may occasionally need small loans for short-term, transitional expenses. Bank loans are expensive and sometimes difficult to get. Create a staff loan policy that will provide small, thirty- to ninety-day loans, no questions asked.

OFFER ANNUAL BONUSES. Once a year, offer small bonuses to each employee. The amount may be negligible, but the impression of caring will go a long way.

REWARD STAFF FOR ACHIEVEMENTS. Give small monetary awards to employees who lose a predesignated amount of weight, quit smoking, stick to an exercise regime, or achieve another personal goal. Their achievement will translate into productivity for the organization.

TO HELL WITH BURNOUT

Typically nonprofit staffs are overworked and underpaid. Frequently they're "sick" and "tired" too. They love their organizations; they volunteer long hours; they trade high salaries for internal satisfaction. They can only keep it up so long. Eventually exhaustion and burnout set it.

Unfortunately, organizations watch burnout occur and do nothing about it. Many actually encourage it by expecting staff to work long hours for the cause. "I was saving the world but losing my family," said one executive director. His board and staff knew it was happening but didn't stop it. They expected him to work that hard. They worked that hard too. After years of not dealing with the exhaustion, both the director and staff lost their morale and their vision. The organization has had to cut back its operation.

Employee burnout, unchecked, is as dangerous as incompetence. Watch for it and reduce it by building revitalizers and rewards into your personnel system.

STAFF SABBATICALS. Send people away for a week or a month to study with an expert in your field, to take a course, to get new ideas. People need to be refreshed. The only requirement should be a minimum of three years of service.

MENTAL HEALTH DAYS. Require staff to take "well" days several times a year. Staff who don't choose their own can be "banned" from work by their supervisor.

ORGANIZATION-PAID COURSEWORK. Nourish your staff by encouraging them to take courses. Pay all or part of their tuition. Mary Kay Cosmetics pays for employee courses based on the grade they earn: one hundred percent for an A or B; seventy-five percent for a C; fifty percent for a D; nothing if the employee fails.

THE GOAL LINE STAND AWARD. Even more than raises, staff members need recognition. They work hard for your organization and they want to know you know it. An award that draws on the football analogy of tough times in the trenches enables you to recognize that staff member who had a tough week but survived. It acknowledges that individuals screw up, suffer defeats, but remain valued and competent.

Each of these suggestions provides a way for you to let your employees know you appreciate them—as human beings, not just as employees. For more suggestions, read the latest best-sellers by business gurus; read *Inc.* and *Fortune* magazines; talk to personnel directors in local corporations. Better yet, think about what you'd like an employer to do for you.

Here are some more simple, inexpensive recognition devices borrowed from the corporate sector and the book *The Financial Post Selects the 100 Best Companies to Work for in Canada.*[8]

- OMARK CANADA, LTD. bolsters its employees' savings plans by matching every employee dollar with fifty cents.

- VANCOUVER CITY SAVINGS CREDIT UNION gives employees a rose on their birthdays and on their anniversary of joining the organization.

- SPEEDY MUFFLER KING sends roses to the spouse of each employee on his or her anniversary. They also offer scholarships for employees' children.

- SHOPPERS DRUG MART managers catch their employees "doing something right." They announce names and good deeds at a quarterly staff meeting. All commended employees are entered in a drawing for a free trip for two to Florida.

TEAMWORK AND DECISION MAKING

Nonprofits tend to plan poorly and decide slowly. Both behaviors are inimical to enterprise. As we've said before, enterprise requires strong organization planning and streamlined decision making. Cultivate these behaviors by systematizing them.

PLAN REGULARLY AND FREQUENTLY. Adopt an annual planning process that begins halfway through the fiscal year. Start the process with several institution-wide meetings at which you develop your large plans for the coming year. Then have each department develop its plan, in detail, to support the organization plan. Finally, merge the department plans into a coordinated, comprehensive, achievable institutional plan. Four months into the plan, update it at both the department and institution levels.

OFFER DECISION MAKING TO AS MANY LEVELS AS POSSIBLE. The people who implement programs are the best able to plan and budget for them. By doing so, they will "buy in" to the goals and work even harder to achieve them.

BUDGET AFTER YOU PLAN. Use the final institutional plan to develop budgets for each department. Budgeting should be the last step in the planning process, and should be completed and approved before the start of the fiscal year.

PRODUCE AND USE MONTHLY FINANCIAL STATEMENTS. They are the only way you'll know if you are deviating from your projections. Follow deviations immediately with midcourse corrections. The end of the year is too late to bring the budget back in line.

IMPLEMENT A THIRTY-/SIXTY-/NINETY-DAY DECISION-MAKING STRUC-TURE. Anything truly worth doing can be decided quickly. Create a timeline for ventures (and all major decisions) based on three thirty-day checkoff points. At the end of each thirty-day period, ask yourself if the data suggests you should go forward or not.

Allow yourself time to properly gather, study, and digest information—but no more than ninety days. By the end of that time you should have enough information to know whether a venture is worth pursuing. You should have done common-sense testing of the idea, gathered information on the industry, developed rough costs and income possibilities, and tested the idea on potential corporate partners. If, armed with that information, you are not compelled to jump headfirst into the project, then don't do it—the benefits probably don't outweigh the risks. Stalling the decision won't change that. Some ideas are meant to be left undone. Better the idea than you.

CHECKLIST: CHARACTERISTICS OF AN ENTREPRENEURIAL NONPROFIT

1. Staff is given responsibility and the power to carry it out.
2. Goals are clear; methods of meeting goals are left to individuals.
3. All staff share the organization's vision, goals, philosophy, and style. They trust each other to implement programs.
4. Criticism is sought—and freely rejected.
5. Staff is ego-healthy, self-confident, and can make decisions quickly. People who lack these attributes don't last long.
6. Staff enjoy being somewhat overwhelmed; they thrive on internally created pressure.
7. There is laughter, rowdiness, and other physical outlets for tension—belying the hard work and high expectations below the surface.
8. Staff meetings are regular, required, and democratic. Everyone shares what they're doing, and usually, food as well. The staff take turns leading the meetings.
9. The organization has a strong culture. People fit or they don't. If they don't, they leave quickly.
10. The organization is predictable in the way people are treated; unpredictable in the new and unusual challenges that lead to quality programs.
11. The organization is not afraid of conflict and tension, but requires staff to offer solutions along with complaints.
12. The organization encourages staff to grow, and to leave when their learning curve has leveled off.

13. Staff are willing to try new things, and not afraid to fail.
14. Staff are passionate about their work and the organization.
15. Staff constantly challenge assumptions, asking, "Why do we do this? Is there a better way?"
16. Problems are seen as opportunities.
17. The staff believe in the enterprise philosophy.
18. There is no tolerance for whiners or wimps.
19. The staff think conceptually *and* in specifics.
20. The organization is seen as an experimental laboratory, always evolving and fostering learning opportunities.
21. The organization hires specific skills on contract instead of putting people on payroll.
22. The organization knows its customers well.
23. The organization has a bias toward being different—and better—than other organizations.
24. The organization works with clients repeatedly, getting them involved so they come back for more.
25. The organization is proactive. It goes to people with an idea rather than waiting for someone to come to them.
26. Organization staffers and management are impatient.
27. They plan ahead and project how each department's plans will affect the others'.
28. They believe that people work best on their own intrests.
29. Managers do "grunt" work at times because it builds an egalitarian culture.
30. All staff—including top managers—work the "front desk" regularly to stay in touch with customers.
31. Praise is sincere and free-flowing.
32. There is no apparent physical hierarchy in the offices.
33. Staff's jobs grow with them. There is no expectation of climbing a job ladder.
34. Managers hire staff who are smarter than they are, looking at applicants' qualities not qualifications.

CHAPTER 37
ENTERPRISE AND THE BOARD

A company is judged by the president it keeps.
—JAMES ROOT HULBERT, AMERICAN EDUCATOR

Along this tree
From root to crown
Ideas flow up
And vetoes down.
—ANONYMOUS

TOP TO BOTTOM PHILOSOPHY

First and foremost: Don't do enterprise if your board doesn't agree. They will kill it—and most likely you—in the process. If they don't buy the concept, educate them. Give them this book. Remind them how much money you need them to raise this year. Wait until a majority of your board members—including the most influential ones—approve the concept before undertaking it.

Even after your board approves, you will need to continue educating them. They will have the same concerns your staff has. They will fear that you will start sacrificing quality for money. They'll fear you'll lose your mission. Answer their concerns just as you do those of staff.

Remind your board of the benefits of enterprise, that enterprise empowers your organization to get its message heard. It generates unrestricted revenue. It enables you to do programs you can't currently afford. Remind them that quality is nonnegotiable and that programs staff will be voices of conscience for all earned income ventures. Use the pictures of your new ventures to infuse the board with the excitement and potential of your vision.

Just as you encourage the expression of staff concerns, encourage your board to question the direction. Don't let their misgivings fester because they can poison the process and the organization.

Use your board enterprise champion to help with the education process. Ask him or her to speak at meetings. Ask this individual to invite board members to breakfast to discuss the new direction. As other members join the team, recruit them to woo the reluctant ones. Like staff, your board will be concerned by change. They may be wary of enterprise not because it's bad, but merely because it's different. As they start seeing results, as they get wowed by your new vision and the broadening of possibilities it brings, most will become as excited about enterprise as your staff.

A few may never adjust. Let them go. Some of your oldest board members may have the hardest time. They've had a hand in creating the organization as it currently is; accepting something different may be too hard. As their terms expire, ask them to leave. That isn't easy, but as with staff, both the organization and the individual will be better off.

RECRUITING NEW BOARD MEMBERS

As board members leave, you have the opportunity to replace them, and that is an empowering opportunity for an entrepreneurial nonprofit. Bring on savvy businesspeople. They will apply their skills to furthering your goals, and you will prove to the world that you do what you say. This is one more opportunity to make your vision and your promise real.

You have told the world you are the best organization in your area of specialty. Now use your board members to prove it. Don't just recruit people locally. Go to the best individuals in your field. If you're as good as you say you are, they'll want to join you. Their names on your board will prove to the world that you are what you promise in your slogan.

We are not suggesting that you recruit a figurehead board. No nonprofit can afford that. You need all your board members to work for you, to apply their skills to your activities, and still, of course, to raise money. We are suggesting you think big. Make a grid of the skills, credibility, and expertise you need to make your vision real. Then go to the best person in each area to fill your needs.

CREATING ADVISORS

Help educate your board and begin the transition to enterprise with a marketing advisory group. This is a team of five to seven people—one key staff person, one key board member, and the balance highly respected talent from areas in which you need expertise, such as marketing of consumer goods, printing, sales, advertising, etc.

Ask them to meet two or three times a year at most, only when you have pressing problems for them to address. Their role is to stretch your problems into opportunities by applying their expertise and guiding your business thinking. Make each meeting an hour and a half and give it a targeted agenda that is sent to them in advance. Encourage their repeat participation by keeping the meetings short and sticking to the agenda.

The marketing advisory group will lend credibility as well as expertise. Your board will be impressed by the involvement of respected business professionals. Their involvement may sway reluctant board members to the enterprise camp and may encourage them to use their own business skills in more entrepreneurial ways. Corporations you approach for partnerships will be impressed at the caliber of business associates you have. Group members may also provide contacts for joint ventures.

The marketing advisory group is also a good way to bring capable businesspeople onto your board. After a year of advising you on enterprise, they will be well cultivated for filling board vacancies.

CHAPTER 38
ENTERPRISE AND FUNDRAISING

Business is a combination of war and sport.
—ANDREA MAUROIS, *THE LIFE OF DISRAELI*

NEW! IMPROVED! FUNDRAISING!

Enterprise does not mean you never have to fundraise again. That skirmish goes on. But it does mean you won't fundraise in quite the same way. Donations may always be an important part of your income pie—but because diversification is the goal, donations should never form as large a part as they do now. You will still talk to corporations and foundations about contributions—but you will talk business first and contributions last. You will talk to them about special projects—ever-conscious that projects will be components of your multiyear vision, not isolated activities. You will talk about general operating support— while inviting them to invest in a diversified, entrepreneurial organization, not asking them to support a worthy cause.

Once you're in the enterprise mode, fundraising becomes one more entre-preneurial activity. It reflects the same proactive vision and carries the same market-minded message as everything else you do. You no longer wait for handouts, you no longer expect things because you are "good," you go to corpo-rations and foundations with an offer of what you can do for them. Your days of sophisticated begging are over.

SHIFTING BETWEEN FUNDRAISING AND ENTERPRISE

Fundraising can mesh with enterprise, carefully and comfortably. The coordina-tion rests on the relationship between your development director and your director of enterprise. These two will need to work closely together. (In very small organizations, where the executive director initially plays both roles, it will be very close indeed!) Planning is critical if the two people are to avoid stepping on each others' toes, and instead, strengthen each others' positions.

The coordination between these two departments begins with your organization's annual plan. Look ahead at the projects you plan to do this year, earned income and not, and decide which corporations and foundations you will approach for each. The lists don't need to be mutually exclusive. You can approach one corporation with both venture and fundraising options (as long as you don't present more than three). In fact, that may improve your chance of getting funds. There will be times when your development director will go alone with only funding options. There will be times when your enterprise director will go alone with only venture possibilities. There will be times when the two will go together with a combined menu of options. The important thing is for them to coordinate their activities. Don't ever be in a position where your development director talks to a corporation about a grant while the enterprise director is grooming the corporation for a venture. Clear communications and mutually agreed upon strategy makes fundraising and enterprise smooth, effective partners. They drive an efficient organization.

Generally when you approach a corporation—even if you're hoping for a straight donation—it makes sense to start with marketing options. You will want to impress the corporation with your business sensibilities. You want to single yourself out from the crowd. If the corporation is uncomfortable with enterprise they can always choose to give you a grant. Nevertheless, you want to give them the choice.

Just as you want to lure donors into becoming members, buyers, and visitors, you want to encourage corporations to broaden their association with you. They may start as funders, but your job is to make them event sponsors, product partners, and service partners. Your goal is to develop a long-term relationship with them in which they invest in your organization multiple times and in multiple ways.

ALWAYS AN EYE ON YOUR VISION

Your fundraising efforts should support your vision. You will spend a lot of time and energy educating the public about who you are, what you do, and where you're going. When you ask them for money, make sure they know how it will speed you to those goals. Use your slogan and visuals in your fundraising brochures. Remind people about the projects you've done and those you plan to do. That makes your vision real to everyone involved. Tie each fundraising effort directly to at least one aspect of your vision so people have a concrete opportunity to help you reach it.

At the Vancouver YWCA, all major fundraising efforts are directed toward their initiative Service 2000, providing services to women in need. To make this clear to the public, the YWCA created a Service 2000 Fund. All money in the fund is used to provide services to women in need. They then created a variety of fundraising vehicles that give different audiences opportunities to contribute to the fund.

One of the vehicles is the annual "Pioneer's Reunion." The reunion taps the nostalgia and altruism of the YWCA's oldest supporters. The YWCA's earliest mission was serving women in need. Many of the men and women who helped it in those days are still around. The reunion offers them a chance to get together, reminisce about the old days, and by contributing to the Service 2000 Fund, insure that their early pioneering goals are still being met.

Another vehicle, the $100 Club, invites a broader audience to contribute to the fund. The club taps people's self-interest as well as their interest in bettering the community. The $100 Club asks members to invest $100 a year for ten years. The money is deposited in the fund, where the principal accrues interest and the interest is used to provide services to women in need. Club members may withdraw their money after five years, however, their accrued interest remains with the fund. Few people will actually withdraw it, and even those who do know they've helped the fund grow.

A third vehicle invites people to "insure" the provision of services to women in need by giving them a chance to purchase a life insurance policy naming the YWCA as beneficiary. A portion of each premium is then donated to the Service 2000 Fund.

Through all these vehicles, the YWCA reminds people about its vision. It offers concrete proof that it is achieving its goals. And it invites multiple audiences to help them do it.

CHAPTER 39
ENTERPRISE AND TAXES

Nothing in life is to be feared. It is only to be understood.
—MARIE CURIE, CHEMIST AND PHYSICIST

MYTH IS A FEMALE MOTH

Myths and fears abound about nonprofits, earned income, and taxes. They're urban legends—like alligators in New York City sewers—that are passed around the country without much basis or documentation. Hopefully, this chapter will lay many of your misconceptions to rest, for while the tax code is complicated, it need not be intimidating. It has a lot of gray area (confusing even to tax attorneys and the IRS). But if you choose to see it as such it can be just as enabling as limiting. So cheer up! What follows is a brief explanation of the aspects of the code that affect nonprofit enterprise.

THE CURRENT TAX CODE

The current IRS code allows nonprofits several avenues for generating nontaxable income. Museums run gift shops and travel programs, hospitals run restaurants and pharmacies, colleges rent dorm rooms and computers, social service agencies sell counseling to corporate employees...and few of them pay tax. As long as a business venture is substantially related to an organization's mission, its income will be exempt. It is possible, legal, and absolutely ethical to earn large amounts of income and not owe any tax. Here's why.

The tax code that governs nonprofit earned income specifies three characteristics a nonprofit activity must meet *in order to be taxable.*

- It must be "unrelated to the organization's tax-exempt mission."

- It must be "regularly carried on."

- It must be deemed a "trade or business."

If an activity meets all three of these criteria, its income will be subject to UBIT—Unrelated Business Income Tax. Few ventures meet all three.

TRADE OR BUSINESS

The "substantially related" test is by far the most important. To be substantially related to an organization's mission, a venture must contribute in an "important way" to the furthering of that mission. It must not exist solely to make money. According to that definition, the operation of an off-campus fast food franchise by a university is not related, but the sale of textbooks is, because textbooks further the university's purpose of educating students.

Income from a catering business run by a history museum is not related, but income from Victorian dinners such as those held at the Molly Brown House in Denver *is* related, because such dinners further the museum's purpose of educating people about history.

To be "regularly carried on," an activity must be ongoing, not occasional. If it is comparable to commercial activity—such as the running of a store—then it is likely to be considered "regularly carried on." By this definition, the operation of a store is regularly carried on; chances are a one-time special event will not be. Obviously many nonprofits generate tax-free income from stores that are regularly carried on. They are able to do so because the stores sell merchandise that is related to their missions, or because they meet one or more of the exceptions explained below.

The purpose of these regulations is not to keep nonprofits from operating a trade or business. Nonprofits can run related businesses that are not taxable. The regulations' purpose is to keep them from running an ongoing business that exists solely to make money and that would compete unfairly with taxable businesses.

Unfortunately (perhaps fortunately!) none of these criteria is absolutely clear. Like many things in law, the code leaves a great deal open to interpretation. This lack of clarity leaves nonprofits a fairly wide berth for operating untaxed earned income activities.

BUSINESS, BUT NOT TAXABLE

A nonprofit can run an unrelated business that is not taxable if the business meets one of the following criteria:

- Is the activity conducted primarily by volunteers? If so, it is probably exempt.

- If the activity involves the sale of merchandise, has substantially all of the merchandise been donated? If so, it is probably exempt.

- Is the activity carried on primarily for the convenience of your members, students, patients, officers, or employees? If so, it is probably exempt.

- Is the activity producing "passive income," such as rents, royalties, or dividends? If so, it is probably exempt.

These exemptions permit many nonprofits to realize substantial untaxed profits from ongoing businesses. Hospitals, for example, earn untaxed income from the portion of their pharmacies that are operated for the convenience of patients.

Service organizations generate untaxed revenue in thrift shops because the thrift shops are run by volunteers and sell merchandise that has been donated.

Museums make untaxed money from restaurants because the restaurants exist for the convenience of museum visitors.

DETOURS AND SHORTCUTS: PROPOSED CHANGES

Because so many nonprofits have made money from untaxed businesses, a coalition of small business owners regularly challenges the IRS code, claiming it is too lenient. They charge that nonprofits compete unfairly with small businesses because they don't pay tax on their revenues. This argument comes center stage or fades from the limelight, depending upon the economic climate in a particular year or even decade. But the fuss over the taxability of nonprofit enterprise never seems to go away.

Much of the focus of such investigations has to do with the "substantially related" test. Congress has tightened the definition of relatedness in recent years, but there is still quite a bit of gray area. Some of those areas include whether there is relatedness of income from affinity credit cards, advertising (especially on the Internet), property rental, and on the nature of nonprofit "subsidiaries." Changes in the tax code are made every year, so our advice remains the same: Stay friendly with a CPA knowledgeable in these areas—and relax.

RELAX

Some possible changes sound ominous, particularly ones that would impact the taxability of your enterprise activities or even threaten your nonprofit classification. But they need not make you nervous for several reasons:

1. All proposed changes in the tax code are not designed to keep nonprofit from earning income. They are designed to keep them from competing

unfairly with taxpaying businesses. The IRS and Congress will continue to address isolated areas of nonprofit activity that compete directly with business, and level the playing field by taxing those activities.

2. Current tax law and proposed changes in it affect only those activities that are unrelated to an organization's mission. That's not what this book is about. If, as our book suggests, you use related earned income ventures to further your goals, taxes will not be an issue. Your ventures, like the ventures described here, will be inherently, purposely, substantially related to your mission.

3. Any changes in the tax code will not threaten an organization's tax-exempt status unless its unrelated income far outweighs its related income. Again, the ventures described in this book are related and should not place an organization at risk.

4. Nowhere in the tax code—current or proposed—does it say a nonprofit can't earn income. The code merely states that unrelated income will be taxed. Yet nonprofits fear taxes as they would a plague. Taxes are just another expense. If you are considering an unrelated venture, calculate the amount of tax you will have to pay on its earnings and include that on the expense side of your pro forma. If the venture still earns a reasonable profit, do it!

5. You can view the tax code as punitive or enabling. If you see it as punitive, you will lament the things you cannot do. Look instead at the things you can do! The range of related activities is tremendous. If you're concerned about the relatedness of a venture you're considering, consult an attorney who is familiar with the code. Make him or her your ally in determining what you can and can't do. If need be, pay tax. The field of nonprofit enterprise is full of possibilities for organizations that are proactive, innovative, and willing to take a calculated risk. Grab the opportunities!

CHAPTER 40
ENTERPRISE AND LESSONS LEARNED FROM LEADERS

There comes a time in every enterprising person's life when they ask, "What the heck am I doing here?" Not to worry. That question just goes with the territory. Your efforts to build enterprise in your organization are breaking new ground. There's bound to be some concern about whether you are doing the right thing.

Who understands your feelings, even the whites-of-your-eyes panic you may be experiencing? The world's greatest entrepreneurs do. Every Internet billionaire, we're willing to bet, has been there. And they have learned some lessons from the business world that apply to your nonprofit organization. Whether you are new to this enterprise thinking or not, take these thoughts to heart because they are borne of a thousand experiences:

- RUN LIKE A BUSINESS ALL THE TIME. Have a separate business board if possible. Insulate enterprise from traditional programs.

- REMEMBER, IT TAKES MONEY TO MAKE MONEY. You can never have too much capital. And there is no substitute for rigorous planning.

- BE COMMITTED TO CONTINUOUS INNOVATION AND IMPROVEMENT. Always compare yourself to your competitors.

- PRODUCE A PREMIUM PRODUCT FOR A PREMIUM PRICE. Your customers must have disposable income. Always separate your clients from your customers.

- ADD VALUE TO EVERYTHING YOU DO. Do things your customers are sure to appreciate.

Along with these lessons, there are also some good questions worth asking. These have been posed by the authors of this book time and time again over three decades. You may not know the answers, but the questions are still worthy of consideration:

1. What can we afford to invest and lose?
2. Would our mission be better served if we did something else?
3. Have we calculated our capital-raising time and costs? And return?
4. Do we have the discipline to protect the business from interference?
5. Do we have the discipline to plan for success, and nurture the business between good and bad times?
6. Do we have the confidence to risk failure?
7. Can we stay in for the long haul?
8. Will our venture detract from the organization's mission and image?
9. Can the venture be embraced by stakeholders?
10. Will operating the business change our culture?

These questions are also worth revisiting on a regular basis. Take a retreat day every six months. Reevaluate. Brainstorm. Stomp around and curse. Become inspired. Asking these questions (and reviewing earlier answers) will help.

So, you have lessons from the business world to help you on your way. You also have questions to help you reflect on your progress. What else can we offer you? How about some good old-fashioned advice? Come here and set a spell on the front porch while we dish up some tried and true wisdom:

- To succeed at enterprise, you must have support from the top: board and top staff. If you don't have it, be careful. The seeds of your great ideas and energy may not have found fertile ground. Not yet.

- Understand that your board can be an incredible asset. Look over their resumes. Where have they been? Sometimes, successful business leaders who are asked to serve on nonprofit boards come alive when asked to advise you or make connections on your behalf. They might surprise you.

- Tough decisions are a given.

- Go after unrestricted operating revenue. If you are dealing with companies who want to put strings on how you use the profits of the partnership, then you aren't equals. You don't tell them what products to sell, now, do you?

- Corporations will challenge you: Know your "walk away" conditions. Even if you have to practice in front of the mirror (which isn't such a bad idea anyway), be ready to courteously stand, shake hands, and say, "I'm sorry, that's not acceptable for us." The first time you do it, it's scary. After that, you realize what power you have over your own destiny (see also Chapter 7 on "Knowing the Lingo/Knowing Your Value").

- And as a related message, this is a give-and-get proposition, not a donor/recipient relationship. You are in business together. So stand tall.

- Invest the time to manage ventures correctly. None of us is proud of haphazard enterprise. It is serious business and deserves your best effort.

- Be attentive to your partner's needs. We are constantly surprised by how many nonprofits do not regularly consider what their partners are looking for in the relationship. Engaging in enterprise partnerships only concerned with your own outcomes is just plain selfish. And it never works out in the long run.

- Know where the money will go. Not only will it communicate to your leadership and to your partners that you have a vision, but you will be energized by the knowledge that this venture will build your dream (or part of it) for the organization.

- Remember that there is enormous potential in what you are doing. Amen.

And, as a closing thought, here are hints from some heavy hitters of social enterprise. The Web sites listed here are (hopefully) going to be around for quite a while and they will link you to resources of almost unlimited potential. The individuals and organizations that provide information to people like you via these Internet sites do indeed know about enterprise. It's a funny thing, too, that they are all wonderful people. Maybe a little pushy now and then, but that's because they know where they are going and they can become impatient with people who don't know the same for themselves. Check these out:

- WWW.COMMUNITYWEALTH.ORG
  This site is run by Community Wealth Ventures, which provides resources to maximize the impact of the nonprofit sector, businesses, and grant-making organizations that are working to strengthen America's communities. It will give you a crash course in best practice and theory of social enterprise.

- WWW.PFDF.ORG
  Year after year, Peter F. Drucker's foundation continues to provide quality resources and educational opportunities to anyone who cares about excellence

in the nonprofit world. Visit descriptions of winners of the annual Peter F. Drucker Award for Nonprofit Innovation and you will surely be inspired.

- WWW.ENTREWORLD.ORG

  A service of the Kauffman Center for Entrepreneurial Leadership, this site will also provide you with resources to develop your enterprise and leadership skills. The focus on critical skills and values for successful entrepreneurship is particularly helpful.

- WWW.REDF.ORG

  The Roberts Enterprise Development Fund shows what can happen when social entrepreneurs have capital available to implement good ideas. The success stories are sure to keep your motivation for successful enterprise high.

- WWW.SURDNA.ORG

  Here is another foundation resource. As Surdna shares its philanthropic goals via this Web site, it communicates what quality social enterprise should include and what should be avoided. They see the "big picture" and that perspective is important when you are focused on your own organization and your perceptions of its limitations.

Know of other great resources? Write or e-mail us (see our addresses on page 227). Watching the spirit of social enterprise grow among our peers is one of the great joys of working with nonprofit organizations and their innovative leaders.

CHAPTER 41
WHAT LIGHT THROUGH YONDER NONPROFIT BREAKS?

There was a young lady named Bright,
Whose speed was far faster than light;
She set out one day
In a relative way,
And returned home the previous night.
—*PUNCH*, DECEMBER 19, 1923

Our society is rapidly changing. From a marketing point of view, we are already well into the new millennium. Business is geared up to sell its dream. From Internet start-up companies to established blue-chip conglomerates, sophisticated psychographic and demographic research continues to drive sales to the hottest new segment of clearly defined target markets.

Do you know where your constituents are tonight? Entrepreneurial nonprofits do. They will be no less amazed at some of the emerging trends as the rest of society, but they won't be surprised by them. Many enterprising nonprofits will harness and set trends themselves. As consumer groups become more splintered, corporations will need to be more proficient at finding them. Your organization can be a great resource for this and an influential social force, too.

Early in this book we discussed creating change rather than watching it. We hope we have offered some tools—and sparked some fantasies—that will assist you in your mission.

Baseball writer Roger Kahn was approached by a disgruntled fan at a minor league game. "They aren't very good," said the fan of the minor league players. "Good enough to dream," replied Kahn.

Are you?

APPENDIX

ENTERPRISE WORKSHEET

This worksheet will help you consolidate the ideas you've gotten from this book into a list of ventures your organization might pursue. If you get stuck while filling it out, or if you come up with an idea you're not sure will work, give us a call, or mail your completed worksheet to us. We'll be happy to help you—for free!

AddVenture Network
1350 Lawrence Street, Plaza H
Denver, Colorado 80204
(303) 572-3333
Fax (303) 572-3355
rsteckel@aol.com

DEFINE YOUR MISSION: NARROWLY AND BROADLY

You're used to defining your mission narrowly. Defining it broadly may help you recognize new areas for action, new audiences to serve, and new partners to work with.

Example: National Crime Prevention Council
narrow mission: to help people protect themselves from crime at home and on the street
broad mission: to help build stronger communities, including fighting child abuse, drug education, involving businesses in protecting their neighborhoods and employees, and building bridges between community groups

DEFINE YOUR MISSION
Narrowly:

_____

_____

227

DEFINE YOUR MISSION
Broadly:

_____
_____
_____
_____

TAKE STOCK OF YOUR ASSETS

List your organization's assets, including credibility, expertise, individual staff skills, physical assets, programs, print and media pieces, etc.

_____
_____
_____
_____
_____

WISH LIST

What programs, products, or services do you wish your organization could do?

_____
_____
_____
_____

TAKE STOCK OF YOUR AUDIENCES

Who do you serve now? (current)

_____
_____
_____
_____
_____
_____

TAKE STOCK OF YOUR AUDIENCES

Who *else* needs or wants what you do? (future)

_____

_____

_____

_____

_____

WHO WANTS TO DO BUSINESS WITH YOU?

What businesses serve the same audiences you do? List them. They are all potential partners because you can help them look good to their customers.

_____

_____

_____

_____

_____

WHAT CAN YOU DO FOR...?

Given your broad mission and assets, what can you do for each of the businesses you've listed above? What kinds of programs, products, or services can you offer that will help them attract customers and spread your message?

_____

_____

_____

_____

_____

WHO NEEDS OR WANTS...?

Look at your assets and wish list again. What businesses might want those things to help build their own business?

_____

_____

_____

_____

_____

REPACKAGING

What do you already have (or do) that, with a little repackaging, might meet a business's need?

_____

_____

_____

_____

_____

_____

_____

ENTERPRISE BLUEPRINT

Fill in the chart below to create an "enterprise blueprint" for your organization.

PRODUCTS	YOUR VENTURE IDEA	AUDIENCE GROUP	CORPORATE BUYERS
Publications			
Tapes			
Kits			
Calendars			
Posters			
Maps			
Special Events			
Instructional Services			
Internet Services			
Others			

PRIORITIZE YOUR VENTURES

Of all the ventures on your chart, which are the easiest to pursue?

- Check the top few against the "nine criteria" (pp. 110–112).

- Choose one or two to start with.

- Establish a thirty-/sixty-/ninety-day decision schedule for those.

ENTERPRISE CALENDAR

TASK	MONTH 1	MONTH 2	MONTH 3
Select an enterprise champion.	X		
Complete your "third-year questions."	X		
Develop your vision statement.	X		
Hire a copywriter to craft your vision slogan.	X		
Hire an artist to illustrate your vision and venture.	X		
Develop a strategy for communicating your vision to multiple publics.		X	
Educate your staff and board about your new direction.		X	
Hire a director of enterprise, and create an enterprise department.		X	
Prioritize your possible ventures according to the nine criteria.		X	
Establish a thirty-/sixty-/ninety-day decision schedule.		X	
By now you should have a proposal circulating for your first venture.			X
By now the spirit of enterprise should be infusing your organization.			X

NOTES

1. Mark H. McCormack, What They Don't Teach You at Harvard Business School (New York: Bantam Books, 1984), p. 27.

2. Brush Nash and Alan Zullo, The Misfortune 500 (New York: Pocket Books, 1988), p. 56.

3. Gunnar Madsen, Richard Greene, and Mark Pritchard, "My Shoes" (Best of Breed Music Publishing, 1986). Used with permission.

4. Initiative on Nonprofit Entrepreneurship, The Nonprofit Venture Reporter (New York: New York University, Fall 1988), p. 2.

5. William Robinson and Robert Rogers, "The Way You Do the Things You Do" (Jobete Music, BMI, 1964). Used with permission.

6. Tom Parker, In One Day (New York: Houghton Mifflin Company, 1984) p. 77.

7. Eva Innes, Robert L. Perry, and Jim Lyon, The Financial Post Selects the 100 Best Companies to Work for in Canada (Toronto, ON: Totem Books, 1986), p. 322.

ABOUT THE AUTHORS

RICHARD STECKEL, the president and founder of AddVenture Network in Denver, has an international reputation as a consultant and speaker on nonprofit marketing and for-profit cause-related marketing. Since 1984, Dr. Steckel has developed earned income strategies, products, and services as an "enterprise coach" for more than one hundred nonprofit and for-profit organizations. He is the author of (with several coauthor partners) *Doing Best by Doing Good, In Search of America's Best Nonprofits,* and *Making Money While Making a Difference.* Before founding AddVenture Network, he was the executive director of the Denver Children's Museum, which became a national model of the earned income approach to fundraising.

ROBIN SIMONS is the author of seven books, including *The Couple Who Became Each Other: Tales of Healing and Transformation,* coauthored with David Calof (Bantam, 1996); *After the Tears: Parents Talk about Raising a Child with a Disability* (Harcourt Brace, 1987); and *Recyclopedia: Games, Science Projects and Crafts from Recycled Materials* (Houghton Mifflin, 1976). Simons worked for many years at the Boston and Denver Children's Museums, as a consultant in museum programming and interactive exhibit design, and as a consultant to the National Endowment for the Arts. Simons lives with her daughter and husband on Bainbridge Island in Washington State.

PETER LENGSFELDER is the consommé writer. His concoctions have satisfied marketing taste-makers and magazine readers alike. Today, his stock and tirade is producing nourishing television in San Francisco, where the fog is often soupy.

JENNIFER LEHMAN of Denver is a senior consultant with AddVenture Network and an advisor to nonprofit organizations across the country. She also works with corporations and philanthropic foundations on strategic planning and innovative marketing. She is the coauthor with Dr. Steckel of *In Search of America's Best Nonprofits.*

INDEX